Reading the Whole Page

Teaching and Assessing Text Features to Meet K-5 Common Core Standards

Michelle Kelley & Nicki Clausen-Grace

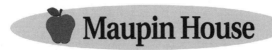

Cover Design: Studio Montage
Book Design and Layout: Rick Soldin

Text features feature images from Okapi Educational Publishing and Rourke Publishing LLC were used with permission.
Maupin House publishes professional resources for K-12 educators. Contact us for tailored, in-house training or to schedule
an author for a workshop or conference. Visit www.maupinhouse.com for free lesson plan downloads.

Library of Congress Cataloging-in-Publication Data

Kelley, Michelle.
   Reading the whole page : teaching and assessing text features to meet K-5 common core standards / Michelle Kelley
& Nicki Clausen-Grace.
      p. cm.
   Includes bibliographical references.
   ISBN 978-1-936700-55-4 (pbk.)
   1. Reading (Elementary)--Activity programs--United States. 2. Reading (Elementary)--Ability testing--United
States. 3. Reading (Elementary)--Standards--United States. I. Clausen-Grace, Nicki. II. Title.
   LB1573.K46 2012
   372.4--dc23   2012010095

ISBN: 978-1-936700-55-4

10 9 8 7 6 5 4 3 2 1

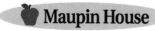 Maupin House

Maupin House Publishing, Inc.
2416 NW 71st Place
Gainesville, FL 32653
www.maupinhouse.com
800-524-0634
352-373-5588
352-373-5546 (fax)
info@maupinhouse.com

Dedication

We dedicate this book to the many teachers who strive to make expository texts enticing and comprehensible for their students. We also dedicate it to the people we love most, our families. To our husbands, Shaun and Jeff, who took over household duties or other family obligations so we could write—we say thanks. To our children, who allowed us writing time and served as sounding boards as we developed lessons—you are the best. To our dogs, who curled by our feet as we typed and became the stars of our e-book—thanks for being there. Without all of you, this book would not be possible.

Acknowledgments

Writing this book has allowed us to get elbow-deep into great non-fiction texts side by side with the students. To Nicki's fourth graders: We appreciate your infectious enthusiasm for learning and your fresh perspectives on what makes text interesting and accessible. Most of all, we enjoyed your excitement about reading and writing non-fiction. You inspire us!

Additionally, several of our co-workers opened their classroom doors, allowing us the pleasure of working with younger students as well. To Sharon Smith, now-retired kindergarten teacher (and suspected fairy godmother): Thanks for showing us just how rigorous and exciting the kindergarten curriculum can be. To Kim Wilson, first-grade teacher extraordinaire: We never left your classroom anything less than amazed by the work you and your students were doing. Nicki can't wait to teach those kids when they get to fourth grade!

To our friend Kim Alloway, a graduate student at the University of Central Florida, who was responsible for translating our vision into an e-book on the CD which is a companion piece with this resource: Kim, you are amazingly talented and generous with your time. Thanks again and again. Also, a special thank you goes to Dr. Marian Cummings, Nicki's former principal, for providing an environment where innovation and collaboration could take root and grow.

Of course, we wouldn't be able to teach about text features without high-quality examples. Thank you to Okapi Educational Publishing and Rourke Publishing LLC for allowing us to share some of the beautiful text features from your trade books.

And finally, without Maupin House, this book would be nothing more than poorly organized sticky notes, spiral notebooks, and our hard drives. A special thanks to Julie Graddy, who envisioned our work as a teaching resource, and especially to Emily Raij, who patiently worked overtime to help us acquire images and make this book teacher friendly. Thanks for helping us create a resource that will help children make sense of and appreciate the text features around them.

Contents

Chapter 4: Organizational Features Mini-lessons 97

Chapter 5: Integrating and Showing Text Feature Knowledge 107

Appendix A: References 115

Appendix B: Common Core Reading Standards Relevant to Teaching Children to Read. 116

Appendix C: Knowledge of Text Features Assessment 123

Appendix D: Suggested Resources for Teaching Text Features. 136

Appendix E: Thinksheets 137

Appendix F: List of Resources on the CD 202

Figures and Tables

Introduction

Peek in the door of a primary classroom during choice reading time and you are likely to see students looking at, talking about, and reading non-fiction books with great enthusiasm. Who wouldn't want to peruse photos of killer creatures in their natural habitats or see pictures of interesting-looking people from around the world?

Left alone, young readers often use these texts like a photo album, ignoring captions and text and letting the pictures tell the story. Unless we teach them *how* to effectively read non-fiction expository text, that in which text features are an integral part, they may never move beyond the "photo album" stage. Ironically, authors use text features to help readers more fully understand the text, but it is these same features that can prove problematic.

Peek in the door of a typical intermediate classroom during choice reading, and you will see a whole lot less non-fiction being read. When these students pick up a book, most leave the non-fiction on the shelf and go for a narrative text. Why does this happen? The complexity of informational text, compounded by the use of text features to convey important information, can sway intermediate students toward fiction for pleasure reading. In our experience, when students are explicitly taught how to read and comprehend non-fiction texts, they understand these texts better, perform better on standardized tests, and are more likely to read them for choice reading.

The idea for this book evolved as we looked at ourselves, our students, and our information-rich world. We are friends, co-authors, and research partners, and we are very different readers. For pleasure reading, Nicki gravitates toward the latest fiction. Michelle is much more likely to be caught reading a journal article in her free time. Working so closely together and both being rather analytical, it didn't take long for us to recognize we attack texts differently. If we are discussing an article or a book about (what else?) teaching, Nicki is usually drawn to the main body of text, while Michelle often is quite taken with the flow charts and tables. Noticing these differences and learning from each other helped us realize that the special skills and knowledge required to read non-fiction expository text can and should be taught.

We all want children to read a wide variety of texts. Reading non-fiction enhances prior knowledge and expands students' vocabulary. Students will not only enjoy these texts now, but are likely to read more of them in their lifetime than narrative fiction. What's more, with the Internet and television, the world our children live in is increasingly graphically oriented. Teaching students to extract the full meaning from images and text is critical to their future success.

What's Included in This Book

The primary goal of this instructional resource is to assist you in teaching your students what a text feature is, how to use it when reading to better comprehend, and how to create it in their writing. In Chapter 1, we touch upon relevant Common Core Standards and grade-level expectations for text features. We then describe the *Knowledge of Text Features Assessment*, which we have developed for students in kindergarten through first grade and in grades two and up. We have also included a class profile, so you can quickly see your students' results at a glance. We created an e-book (found on the CD), which can be printed or used on a computer to assist when giving this assessment, although other texts can be used. Depending on how your students do on the *Knowledge of Text Features Assessment* and/or your teaching standards, you will be able to dip in and out of chapters based on your students' needs. This will allow you to appropriately differentiate instruction.

This lofty goal is possible with the lessons in Chapters 2 through 4 and your thoughtful instruction. The lessons follow a gradual release of responsibility model (Pearson & Gallagher, 1993), with the beginning lessons being more teacher-directed and the final lessons requiring students to demonstrate knowledge of the feature being taught. Within each of these chapters, the lessons are loosely hierarchical, with the more primary ones listed first.

In Chapters 2 through 4, we have categorized text features as either print features (those that support the reader mainly through print), graphic features (those that support the reader mainly through images), or organizational features (those that help the reader navigate the organization of the text). Chapter 2 includes lessons on print features, Chapter 3 has lessons on graphic features, and Chapter 4 contains lessons on organizational features. When logical, we have combined lessons for features with similar purposes, such as drawings and photographs.

Prior to lessons in each chapter, you will find mini-introductions for the features targeted in that chapter. Each lesson then follows a predictable format. The lesson title, purpose, and materials are listed at the beginning. The directions open with a little teacher talk explaining the feature to students. Feel free to use our words as a script or just a reference, depending on your comfort level. These lessons have students seeing and exploring text feature examples and manipulating or creating text features on their own. Each lesson closes with a review of what was learned, modifications for younger or less-able students, assessment options, and technology connections.

Ultimately, we want students to integrate their knowledge of all text features when reading. Chapter 5 contains tried and true activities to help them do so. These include the text feature walk, creating class books, and conducting text feature scavenger hunts developed to help students put together their text feature knowledge.

Our appendices include helpful and important resources referenced throughout this book. The CD has printer-friendly versions of these resources, as well as lesson supports (such as the thinksheets referred to in lessons) to facilitate implementation, examples of each text feature, the picture book used for assessment purposes (and described in more detail in Chapter 1), to allow for more student engagement. To assist readers in assimilating their knowledge of text features learned and sharing this knowledge with other students, a readers' theatre script has been developed for each of the text feature chapters (print, graphic, and organizational) and is included on the CD.

Also included on the CD are interactive versions of Thinksheets that you and your students can fill out directly on a computer using Adobe Acrobat. Look for this icon () on the Thinksheets in Appendix E and in the CD listing at the end of this book to see which files are interactive.

Chapter 1
The Importance of Teaching Text Features Explicitly

Listen in on these fourth graders involved in a text feature walk, an informational text-previewing technique similar to a picture walk. Mixed-ability students in small groups scattered throughout the classroom have their social studies textbooks open as they discuss the text features on the first page of the text.

After reading the chapter title, a student says, "'The Earliest Floridians.' So I think this is going to be about the Indians who first lived here."

Another student chimes in, "I think so, too ... I see a picture of a spear, and last year we talked about Indians in Florida using spears."

Another student points and says, "There is a huge drawing of an early native right here. He has a necklace on made of pearls—that's weird."

"I don't think those are pearls. I think they are shells or rocks. I know they used rocks and shells to make their spears. I think we are going to learn about how they used the spears as tools."

"Yeah, I think we are going read how they used spears and the different ways they used them."

These fourth graders accessed background information, made connections to previous learning, clarified ideas in the text, and anticipated what they were going to read and learn about. This is powerful stuff. But it didn't just happen. It all started earlier in the year, and it is the result of teaching non-fiction text features explicitly.

If students are to successfully navigate informational texts, they must understand text features—the components of a text that are not considered its main body. These include the table of contents, glossary, headings, bold words, pictures and captions, and labeled diagrams, among others. If these features are clearly presented, concise, and related to the content, they can help the reader. On the other hand, they can impair comprehension if they are poorly organized, only loosely related to content, or too wordy.

Key to Comprehension

If you are like us, it is likely some of your students skip over a title or heading when reading informational text. Undoubtedly, you have also had a student pass over an important picture and caption or a diagram that explained something critical. Or, perhaps a student has also asked you a question about the text which was answered in a text feature he failed to read or consider.

Despite the importance of text features to understanding informational text, researchers have found that most students pay little or no attention to them. Hannus and Hyona (1999) used eye-movement technology and determined that elementary students spent just six percent of their total reading time viewing graphics in text and that the readers who would benefit the most from reading these features typically ignored them completely.

Even if students pay attention to text features, many find them confusing or don't fully realize their value when reading (Barton, 1997).

McTigue and Flowers (2011) provide an overwhelming argument for the need to teach children how to read and learn from science text features, specifically graphics. Their review of recent research and analysis of the use of graphics in science texts points not only to an increase in the usage of graphics in texts, but also an increase in the variety of graphics, as many features are hybrids of multiple text features. Moreover, these authors point out that most texts offer readers little support to help them decipher these features in order to better access the content.

Additionally, text features are being assessed more frequently on state and national tests. Yeh and McTigue (2009) found that half of the questions in the high-stakes science assessments in grades four and up contain graphics features and that eighty percent of these have essential information required for the student to respond accurately.

And, of course, the knowledge, use, and application of text features are prevalent throughout the Common Core Standards, so students will inevitably be held accountable for demonstrating these skills while reading and discussing what they have read.

Table 1.1 (pages 117–122) in **Appendix B** highlights the K-5 Common Core Reading Standards that are relevant to teaching children text features across the curriculum and which are taught in this resource. Although many of these standards do not name a specific text feature, using text features will help students accomplish the standards. For example, in the Reading Standards for Informational Text (K-5), under "Craft and Structure," second-grade students are to: "Determine the meaning of words and phrases in a text relevant to a grade 2 topic or subject area." Noticing bolded and italicized words and using a glossary will assist with accomplishing this standard.

Explicitly Teaching Text Features

After working with students, perusing children's non-fiction texts, and reflecting on our own reading and teaching processes, three major categories of text features emerged: print, graphic, and organizational. With a print feature, the actual text of the feature supports the reader, such as a title or a heading. Organizational features, such as a table of contents or an index, also occur primarily in print, but it is the structure of the feature, not only the text, that supports the reader's journey. In contrast, graphic features, such as a diagram or a map, are image-based. They may or may not include print as a component, but it is the image itself and the way it is presented that help the reader understand the text.

These text feature categories help us identify a common language for explicit instruction, a major challenge to teaching them. Helping students to read and understand text features as they relate to the main idea of a text is one powerful way to improve comprehension. This begins by first identifying the text feature and its purpose. Then teachers can model and explain through think-alouds how readers gain information from the feature. This will help students see what a proficient reader does before, during, and after reading.

Demonstrating how to preview sections of text using the text features will help readers anticipate and discuss what they are going to read and learn. With academic discussion an essential component of standards-based reading instruction, it is important for students to discuss why the author may have chosen to use a specific feature and where it was positioned in the text. Eventually, we want students to use these features in their own writing.

So why are some text features so difficult for students to decipher and use? To begin with, students must comprehend concepts from both the text and graphic, then determine how the two are related, and decide whether the information is pertinent to the text. When reading a diagram, students must decide in what order the pictures should be studied and then integrate this with the information in the rest of the text. So what can teachers do to facilitate informational text reading?

They can teach text features explicitly. They can use mini-lessons as they conduct small- and large-group discussions with informational texts or as stand-alone lessons. This resource provides K-5 teachers with guidance to support teaching non-fiction text features as a part of reading instruction in a comprehensive, explicit, and meaningful way.

Bryce (2011) and other researchers suggest that "teachers must consciously provide guidance and support for mining the textbooks for content-area understanding" (p. 483) by explicitly teaching students how to navigate through textbooks. Bryce calls for a "meaning-based pedagogy" in order "to ensure that primary-grade learners benefit from a recognition that textbooks are potentially rich resources for learning about the world" (p. 483). The mini-lessons in this resource will help you accomplish this lofty goal as you successfully teach to the standards.

What Are Text Features and How Do They Help Readers?

Other than a bevy of one-shot text feature activities, we have seen little guidance for teaching non-fiction features in a comprehensive and meaningful way. Teaching text features can be quite challenging without establishing a common language. Since many of us were not taught about these features when we were in school, we felt it would be helpful to not only classify and define common text features in print, but also show an example of each and explain how the feature assists readers.

Table 1.2 defines each text feature, explains how it assists readers, and shows an example of each. Visual examples of each of the text features can also be found in the assessment picture book on the CD and, of course, gleaned from a content-area text or trade book. The CD also includes Table 1.2 with the visual examples.

Table 1.2: **Text Feature Definitions and Examples**

Type of text feature and definition	How this feature helps readers	Visual example of feature
Print Features		
Title The name of a text located on the front cover or at the beginning of a chapter	Indicates the topic and/or main idea of the entire text	 From *Full Throttle*, page 1, Rourke Educational Publishing
Heading/Subheading A secondary heading that divides a section of text; sometimes differentiated from a title by font color	Indicates the main idea of a section of text	 From *Wedges*, page 4, Rourke Educational Publishing
Bold Print Words written in a dark and thick print within the main body of text; often, these words are also defined in the glossary	Signals important vocabulary and/or a phrase that is integral to understanding the content of the text	 From *Wedges*, page 4, Rourke Educational Publishing
Italics Font slanted to the right within the main body of text	Indicates important vocabulary or that the reader should emphasize this word when reading	
Caption Text located near a graphic feature (such as a picture, map, diagram, etc.) that explains what it is	Explains the graphic feature it is nearest to	 From *Full Throttle*, page 19, Rourke Educational Publishing

Type of text feature and definition	How this feature helps readers	Visual example of feature
Pronunciation Guide A phonetic representation of a word usually located in parentheses after the word has appeared in the text	Shows the reader how to pronounce a new or unusual word	**Glossary** 〔pronunciation guide〕 effort (EF urt) — force need... force (FORS) — an action that moves something inclined plane (in KLINED PLANE) — a sloping surface that makes work easier wedge (WEJ) — a simple machine which cuts, divides, splits, or holds something together From *Wedges*, page 23, Rourke Educational Publishing
Bullets Listed text that is indented and aligned using a dot, symbol, or dash in front of each idea	Emphasizes and condenses key points in a text	**Fast Off The Drawing Board** 〔bullet〕 Ford engineers used advanced computer testing to cut two years off the time it usually takes to move a car from the drawing board to production. • **2002** - The new Ford GT **concept car** first dazzled fans at the North American Auto Show. • **2003** - Prototypes rolled out in time for Ford's centennial parade. • **2004** - Production started and Ford delivered From *Full Throttle*, page 11, Rourke Educational Publishing
Sidebar Additional text (not the main body of text) within a box, often with a shaded background; located at the sides, top, or bottom of a page	Provides additional details, facts, or information related to the text	〔sidebar〕 Frank Hurley, photographer, wrote in his diary, "The ship groans and quivers, windows splinter, whilst the deck timbers gape and twist…" After the ship was crushed and the expedition was ... From *Amazing Journeys*, page 13, OkapiExplorations Series, Okapi Educational Publishing
Graphic Features		
Photograph (with or without caption) Picture taken by a camera; captions explain what is shown in photos	Helps the reader visualize real events, steps, or objects described in the text	rockers. They're tuned into a stereo that can blast louder than the eight-cylinder powerhouse—but who really wants to block out that beastly purr? 〔photograph〕 *Holes in those fine leather seats serve a real purpose. The ventilated pattern helps cool* From *Full Throttle*, page 19, Rourke Educational Publishing
Drawing (with or without caption) A hand-created sketch; captions explain what is in the drawing	Helps the reader visualize and better understand something from the text	

Type of text feature and definition	How this feature helps readers	Visual example of feature
Inset A small photo, picture, or map inside or next to a larger picture; insets magnify a part of the larger picture	Helps the reader visualize something in the text in both large and small scale, in combination with the larger picture	This is the Castillo de San Marcos fort (above). It is the oldest Spanish building in Florida. It is 339 years old! This is a close up of a cannon that they shot cannonballs with (above right).
Cross-section A picture of a person, place, or thing that has been cut completely in half, with the open half facing forward so the entire inside of is revealed	Allows the reader to visualize all the layers of a person, place, or thing in the text	
Cutaway A picture of an object with part of the side dissolved, partially revealing the inside	Allows the reader to visualize both the interior and exterior of a person, place, or thing in the text	
Diagram A series of pictures with captions showing steps, stages, or the progression of events	Explains steps in a process or how something is made	Life cycle of the monarch butterfly — eggs, caterpillar, pupa – early stage, pupa – later stage, adult butterfly From *Amazing Journeys*, pages 4–5, Explorations Series, Okapi Educational Publishing
Labeled Diagram A picture with labels on lines pointing to various parts	Shows the different components of something in the text	Petal, Leaf

Type of text feature and definition	How this feature helps readers	Visual example of feature
Map An aerial-view picture showing the geographic location of something or someone	Shows where something or someone is located, as well as trends for a geographic area, like population; helps readers quickly understand the relative location or impact of something in the text	
Graph Data in diagram form such as a bar graph, line graph, or pie graph	Condenses data and/or displays numeric information important to the text; can be used to compare amounts or show changes over time	
Chart/Table Large amounts of information or data organized and condensed into columns and rows with headings	Allows the reader to easily read and compare data related to the text	
Timeline Events listed in linear format in the order that they occur	Allows the reader to understand when events in the main body of text occurred relative to other events	
Organizational Features		
Table of Contents Located at the beginning of the text and lists key topics in the book with the page number in the order they are presented	Helps the reader quickly find the topic he/she is seeking	 From *Wedges*, page 3, Rourke Educational Publishing

Type of text feature and definition	How this feature helps readers	Visual example of feature
Index Located at the back of the book, specific topics, events, names, and terms listed in alphabetical order with page numbers; more specific than the table of contents	Helps the reader quickly find where the specific information he/she is seeking is located	**Index** axe 12 cut 4, 8, 12, 14, 15, 16, 22, 23 saw 14 scissors 12 teeth 14, 22 *From Wedges, page 24, Rourke Educational Publishing*
Glossary Located at the back of the book, an alphabetical listing of text-important words with definitions and sometimes a pronunciation guide; usually, the words in the glossary are bolded in the main body of the text	Helps readers understand new or text-critical words; definitions can be easily found	**Glossary** effort (EF urt) — force needed to insert a wedge force (FORS) — an action that moves something inclined plane (in KLINED PLANE) — a sloping surface that makes work easier wedge (WEJ) — a simple machine which cuts, divides, splits, or holds something together *From Wedges, page 23, Rourke Educational Publishing*

Knowing Where to Start Your Teaching: Assessing Students' Knowledge of Text Features

We recognize that we are living and teaching in a climate of high-stakes assessment. Accountability is the name of the game. We also feel that our students are being over-assessed in many aspects of literacy. So why assess text features? We've already established that students are being tested on their knowledge and use of text features in assessments and that the Common Core Standards require us to teach text features—so teachers need to know what students know (and don't) about text features. Unfortunately, there are only a few informal assessments on the subject—those that guide our teaching and those that help us prepare students for formal assessments. And the informal assessments that do assess text features usually only highlight a few text features, such as titles, maps, and bolded words.

This gap in the field led us to develop a tool, the *Knowledge of Text Features Assessment*, to help you better understand what each student knows and doesn't know when it comes to text features. This assessment not only serves as a pre-assessment to direct your teaching, but also as a progress monitor and a formative assessment so that you can determine if your teaching has been effective.

In addition, we have established end-of-grade-level expectations for text feature knowledge. These end-of-grade-level expectations were created based on a review of the Common Core Standards, our personal teaching experiences, and meetings with elementary teachers at various grade levels (see Table 1.3 and on the CD). These expectations can serve as an instructional guide as you determine what text features your students need to know by the end of the school year and—just as important— what they will be expected to know in the next grade level.

Table 1.3: **Text Feature Grade-level Expectations**

*Note: These are the features to be known by the end of the grade level indicated.

Text Features End-of-grade-level Expectation	K	1	2	3	4	5
Print Features						
Title	✗	✗	✗	✗	✗	✗
Heading		✗	✗	✗	✗	✗
Subheading				✗	✗	✗
Bold Print		✗	✗	✗	✗	✗
Italics			✗	✗	✗	✗
Caption	✗	✗	✗	✗	✗	✗
Pronunciation Guide		✗	✗	✗	✗	✗
Bullets			✗	✗	✗	✗
Sidebar			✗	✗	✗	✗
Graphic Features						
Photograph	✗	✗	✗	✗	✗	✗
Drawing	✗	✗	✗	✗	✗	✗
Inset	✗	✗	✗	✗	✗	✗
Cross-section/Cutaway			✗	✗	✗	✗
Diagram		✗	✗	✗	✗	✗
Labeled Diagram		✗	✗	✗	✗	✗
Map		✗	✗	✗	✗	✗
Graph		✗	✗	✗	✗	✗
Timeline		✗	✗	✗	✗	✗
Chart/Table		✗	✗	✗	✗	✗
Organizational Features						
Table of Contents	✗	✗	✗	✗	✗	✗
Index		✗	✗	✗	✗	✗
Glossary		✗	✗	✗	✗	✗

Knowledge of Text Features Assessment **Overview**

We developed the *Knowledge of Text Features Assessment* to help you determine what individual children know about specific text features. The features in this assessment are categorized as print, graphic, or organizational, which aligns with our end-of-year grade-level expectations. This assessment moves from the identification of text features to reading and using text features to assist with comprehension.

It isn't an absolute necessity to assess your entire class to determine which features you should teach. But, if you feel the need to gather data to show both need and growth through the teaching of text features, the *Knowledge of Text Features Assessment* is very helpful. We offer two versions of this assessment: one for kindergarten through first grade and one for grades two and up. The kindergarten-through-first-grade version assesses only those features which should be known by the end of first grade, while the grade-two-and-up version assesses all features expected to be known by the end of third grade. All of the text features included in this assessment are included in the Common Core Standards and in most state benchmarks. It is expected that by third grade, students will not only be able to name a text feature, but also understand how that feature helps them as readers and then apply this knowledge when reading and writing. The directions for the assessment and the score sheets for each version are located in **Appendix C** (pages 123–135) and on the CD.

Knowledge of Text Features Assessment Picture Book and Other Materials

Since it is hard to find a text that has all of the features on our assessment, we developed an e-book which has all of the assessed text features whether you are assessing primary or intermediate students. On the CD, we have included a PowerPoint version of the book, which can be viewed on any computer, as well as a PDF version, which can be printed as a book. If you choose to print the book, we recommend printing in color.

If you do not choose to use the book we have created for students for the grade-two-and-up assessment, it would also be appropriate to select a non-fiction text that has many or all of the text features on the assessment. A content-area textbook for your grade level would work well. If you are not utilizing the picture book (printed or on the computer), you may have to use more than one book or text in order to assess all of the text features on the assessment. The text selected should be developmentally appropriate, and you can differentiate the text based on a child's interests and experiences. For example, if you are using a science textbook you can point out a few topics and ask the student which topic he would like to read about, and then use this section of text for the assessment.

If you choose not to utilize the e-book on the CD, the text selected should contain examples of the following categories and text features:

- **Print features:** Titles, headings/subheadings, bold print, italics, captions, pronunciation guide, bullets, and sidebars
- **Graphic features:** Photographs with or without captions, drawings with or without captions, insets, cross-sections/cutaways, labeled diagrams, diagrams, maps, graphs, timelines, and charts/tables
- **Organizational features:** Table of contents, index, and glossary

Giving the Assessment

How you give the assessment should be based on the grade level you teach and the teaching goals you have established for the year. You can choose to give the assessment in segments, such as just the print features section, or all at once. The following snapshot, Figure 1, shows you an example of the kindergarten and first-grade score sheet, where the teacher records a student's text feature knowledge. We have pointed out the teacher prompts that are asked to encourage a student to identify a text feature, share its purpose, and then apply this knowledge in the context of reading. The only

Figure 1: **K-1 *Knowledge of Text Features Assessment* Score Sheet**

K-1 *Knowledge of Text Features Assessment* Score Sheet

Student _____   Grade _____   Date _____

Assent Script: *"Today I am going to ask you to identify some text features. A text feature is anything that is not in the main body of the text, like a title or a picture. I will also ask you to tell me what you know about each text feature. The text feature may be anywhere in the book, so you can look throughout the book to find the text feature. What I learn from this assessment will help me plan instruction to help you be a better reader."*
Optional: *"You will not be graded on this assessment but I do want you to try your best so I can know how to better help you grow as a reader."*
Directions: Place a 0 for no or incorrect response; place a 1 for a correct response.

#	Text Feature *CD picture book page listed*	Teacher Prompt for Identification	Response Score	Teacher Prompt for Purpose	Response Score	Teacher Prompt for Application	Response Score
				PRINT FEATURES			
1	**Title** *Front Cover*	"Show me the title of this book/chapter." If student cannot identify, point to an example.	!	"Why does an author give a book a title?" Possible student response: Tells topic and/or main idea of the entire text		"Read the title and tell me what you think you are going to learn about."	
2	**Heading/ Subheading** H-p.2,36,7,10 SH- p.4,8,9	"Show me a heading/subheading in this book." If student cannot identify, point to an example.	!	"Why does an author give a heading/ subheading?" Possible student response: Tells the main idea of a section of text		"Read the heading/subheading and tell me what you think you are going to learn about."	
3	**Bold Print** p. 3,7,8	"Show me bold print." If student cannot identify, point to an example.	!	"Why does an author use bold print?" Possible student response: Shows important vocabulary in the text		"Read the bold print and tell me what you expect to learn about."	

difference between the kindergarten/first-grade score sheet and the grade-two-and-up score sheet is the number of text features assessed.

In Figure 2 (page 12), we have an example of a fourth-grade student's score sheet from part of the graphic features section. Looking at this, the teacher might notice that this student has no previous knowledge of insets, cross-sections, cutaways, or diagrams. Even though he could identify a map, he did not know its purpose related to the text or how to use the map to gather information. Because there are many kinds of maps used in the social studies textbook, this teacher may decide to target maps in text first. She might also choose to focus on diagrams because they will be studying the rock cycle later in the year and she knows there will be diagrams in the science text.

Knowledge of Text Features Assessment Class Profile

Once you have assessed your students using the score sheet for your grade level, you can plot your entire class onto one of the class profile forms located in **Appendix C** (pages 123–135) and on the CD. The class profile allows you to see at a glance your class's strengths and needs related to text features. You can quickly determine whether you would teach a specific text feature to the whole class or in a small guided-reading group.

Of course, you should also consider your required district and state standards, as well as desired outcomes, when making a decision about what to teach. For example, if students will be expected to coordinate information from the main body of text, a picture and caption, and a sidebar for a graded or standardized task, it makes sense to focus on these text features. Primary students as well as many

Figure 2: **Snippet of *Knowledge of Text Features Assessment*—Grade Two and Up**

1=Correct Response   0=Incorrect Response

	GRAPHIC FEATURES						Response Score
9	**Photograph with or without caption** p.2,3,7-11	"Show me a photograph." If student cannot identify, point to an example.	1	"Why does an author put a photograph in a book?" Possible student response: Helps you see real events, steps, or objects described in the text	1	"Look at the photograph and explain why you think this is in the text/chapter/book."	1
10	**Drawing with or without caption** p.9	"Show me a drawing." If student cannot identify, point to an example.	1	"Why does an author put a drawing in a book?" Possible student response: Helps you see something from the text	1	"Look at the drawing and explain why you think this is in the text/chapter/book."	1
11	**Inset** p.9	"Show me an inset." If student cannot identify, point to an example.	0	"Why does an author put an inset in a book?" Possible student response: Helps you see something in the text in large and small scale	0	"Look at the inset and explain why you think this is in the text/chapter/book."	1
12	**Cross-section/ Cutaway** p.9	"Show me a cross-section or cutaway." If student cannot identify, point to an example.	0	"Why does an author use a cross-section/ cutaway in a book?" Possible student response: Helps you see all the layers or the interior and exterior of a person, place, or thing in the text	1	"Look at the cross-section/cutaway and explain why you think this is in the text/chapter/book."	1
13	**Diagram** p.7,9-9	"Show me a diagram." If student cannot identify, point to an example.	0	"Why does an author put a diagram in a book?" Possible student response: Explains steps in a process or how something is made	0	"Read the diagram. What did you learn?"	1

intermediate students can often use more direct instruction in understanding how a title or table of contents can help them anticipate what they will read. Using these considerations as well as the class profile will help you get the most out of your instruction.

In Figure 3, we have included an example of a first-grade class profile.

Analysis of Sample Class Profile

Looking at this class profile, the highlighted cells are those features students did not know at one or more of the levels of knowledge related to text features (ability to identify a text feature, knowing the purpose of the text feature, and/or using the text feature to aid with comprehension). The class strengths were related to title, bolded print, photographs, maps, timelines, and tables of contents. A closer examination of headings/subheadings tells us that most students know the purpose and can apply heading knowledge but they could not identify it by name. This could be because the class may not have a common language for this feature. A quick review of terminology may be all that is needed for this feature.

For instruction, a first-grade teacher looking at this profile might decide to focus several whole-group lessons on insets because only two of her students could even identify this feature and it appears often

Figure 3: Sample Completed *Knowledge of Text Features Assessment* Class Profile

K-1 *Knowledge of Text Features Assessment* Class Profile

Teacher's Name _____   Grade 1st gr.   Date April 2012

Students' Names	Print Features					Graphic Features								Organizational Features		
	Title	Heading/ Subheading	Bold Print	Caption	Pron. Guide	Photo	Drawing	Inset	Diagram	Labeled Diagram	Map	Graph	Timeline	TOC	Index	Glossary
Zack	IPA	PA	IPA	IPA	PA	IPA	IP	A	A	A	IPA	I	IA	IPA	I	IPA
Ginny	IPA	PA	IPA	IPA	IA	IPA	I	IP	IA	A	IA	IPA	IA	IPA	PA	IA
MacKenzie	IPA	PA	IPA	IPA	A	IPA	PA	(○)	A	PA	IP	P	P	IPA	IPA	I
Danny	IPA	PA	IPA	I	PA	I	A	A	A	IPA	IPA	A	IPA	IPA	IA	IPA
Mike	IPA	PA	P	I	A	IPA	I	A	A	P	PA	(○)	IPA	IA	(○)	(○)
Paul	IPA	PA	IPA	PA	A	IPA	A	P	A	A	IPA	PA	IPA	IPA	PA	IPA
Alec	IPA	PA	IPA	A	(○)	IPA	IPA	A	IPA	IPA	IPA	P	A	IPA	I	(○)
Katie	IPA	A	IPA	A	A	IA	IA	A	IA	IPA	IPA	IPA	IPA	PA	IA	A
Tyler	IPA	PA	IPA	IPA	A	IPA	IPA	(○)PA	IPA	IPA	IA	I		IPA	PA	IPA
Michelle	IPA	P	IPA	IPA	A	IPA	A	PA	(○)	IPA	IPA	I		IPA	IPA	IPA
Kara	IPA	PA	IPA	IP	A	I	PA	P	IA	PA	IA	A		IPA	IPA	A	I
Sari	IPA	PA	IPA	PA	A	IPA	IPA	(○)	A	PA	IPA	IPA	IPA	IPA	IA	IPA
Daver	IPA	PA	IPA	IP	A	IPA	PA	(○)	A	PA	IPA	IPA	IPA	IPA	IA	IA
Sam	IPA	PA	IPA	IPA	A	IPA	PA	A	PA	IPA	A	IPA	IPA	PA	IPA
Toni	IPA	PA	IPA	IPA	A	IPA	IPA	A	PA	IPA	A	IPA	IPA	A	IPA
Suri	IPA	PA	IPA	IPA	A	IPA	PA	(○)	A	IPA	(○)	IPA	IPA	PA	IA
# who identify:	16	(○)	15	12	1	16	8	2	4	4	15	7	14	15	7	13
# who know purpose:	16	15	16	12	2	13	10	4	2	11	14	7	11	15	8	8
# who apply:	16	15	15	12	15	14	13	7	14	14	15	11	13	16	13	12

Key: I = Identifies; P = Knows Purpose; A = Applies

in primary non-fiction texts and weekly periodicals. She might also decide to focus some whole-group lessons on diagrams and labeled diagrams because the state curriculum calls for students to learn about cycles as they relate to science, such as life cycles.

Furthermore, she should probably be concerned about the four students who could not identify a caption or explain why authors use a caption. She might choose to pull these students into a small, guided-lesson group. She will be sure to work with them until they can identify and explain the purpose of a caption, perhaps having students create their own captions to go with a photograph or drawing.

Only one out of sixteen students could identify a pronunciation guide, and only two understood the purpose, but fifteen could use a pronunciation guide to figure out a word. Probably a quick, whole-class lesson on this would help students be more metacognitive about pronunciation guides. As these readers get into more complicated text with multisyllabic vocabulary, they may need to use a pronunciation guide to help them say a word.

Of course, no one would focus on all of these text features at one time. The teacher must prioritize which features to focus on first and determine the depth she wants to go with the features taught.

When Do I Teach Text Features?

The typical ninety-minute reading block usually includes time for whole-group instruction, time for small-group instruction, and time for some type of independent practice. The lessons in the book can be used in all of these ways. Initially, you will want to introduce any new text features to your entire class as a whole-group lesson. This may be followed up with independent or paired practice in reading or writing the feature being taught. Use the lessons in small groups for students who need extra support or when only a few students need instruction on a particular feature. Consider using some of the lessons as a literacy center. For example, have students read through a basket of books about a topic you are studying in science and create a text feature you have studied to show what they learned as they read. You might spend thirty minutes on a whole-group lesson on text features, then transition to a thirty-minute, small, guided-group lesson on the same feature. Students not engaged in the lesson would work in literacy centers, which could also use previously taught lessons on text features.

For older students. In a fourth-grade classroom, the teacher might begin with a think-aloud to introduce insets. She defines the feature, shows examples, and does the first lesson with her whole class. As she transitions into working with a small group, she might have the students she is not working with search their social studies textbooks for examples of insets, either independently or in pairs. One of the literacy centers students might work at during this time could be using an interactive whiteboard to match insets to their bigger picture (see the interactive PowerPoint lesson on insets located on the CD). In a small group, the teacher might have students reading a non-fiction text that includes an inset. She can guide their conversation around how and why this feature is used.

For younger students. In contrast, a primary teacher might choose to do a brief, whole-group, introductory lesson for titles. Students wouldn't be expected to work independently on this feature the first day, so the teacher might move the practice activity to her small group. As students gain familiarity, she can transition one of the activities, such as the "Chapter Title Sort," (included in Chapter 2) to a literacy center.

Now that you have learned how to integrate the teaching of text features into your daily instruction, given the assessment, and reviewed your class profile, you can begin to choose the lessons that are the best fit for your students.

Chapter 2
Print Features Mini-lessons

Overview for Teaching Print Features

You can almost see the light bulb turn on above a child's head when he realizes the title of a book tells him what it is about. Something this basic seems obvious to us as teachers, especially since we spend time talking about and predicting based on the title every time we read with children. But it is a true epiphany for some of our students when they first realize that *all* titles are designed to tell what a book is about.

Print features are special types of text within a piece that help readers comprehend. They serve as a kind of roadmap for readers indicating things like, "Look here! This is the main idea," and, "You'll find information about alligator tails in this section." They help us pronounce unfamiliar words and notice important information.

Print features include titles, chapter titles, headings, bold print, italics, sidebars, pronunciation guides and bullets. If left to their own devices, most young readers simply ignore these unique types of text. To get students to read and rely on print features, we need to move beyond pointing them out in text to guiding students as they use them to support comprehension. Ultimately, we want our children to use these features as independent readers and in their writing as well. The activities in this chapter will help them do just that.

The table below lists the features and lessons taught in this chapter and the grade level(s) when these features should be mastered.

Figure 4: **Print Features End-of-grade-level Expectations and Lessons Related to Each Text Feature**

PRINT FEATURES End-of-grade-level Expectations and Lessons Related to Each Text Feature	K	1	2	3	4	5
Titles	✗	✗	✗	✗	✗	✗
Chapter Title Sort . . . . p. 18 What Comes First? . . . . p. 20 Create a Cover (also helpful for TOC) . . . . p. 21						
Headings		✗	✗	✗	✗	✗
Headings Help Us . . . . p. 23						
Subheadings – see "Titles, headings, and subheadings"			✗	✗	✗	✗

Continued

PRINT FEATURES End-of-grade-level Expectations and Lessons Related to Each Text Feature	K	1	2	3	4	5
Bold Print	✗	✗	✗	✗	✗	✗
Italics		✗	✗	✗	✗	✗
Noticing Bold and Italic Print . . . . p. 25						
Bold and Italic Detective . . . . p. 26						
Captions	✗	✗	✗	✗	✗	✗
What Is a Caption? . . . . p. 28						
Where Does It Fit? . . . . p. 30						
How Does It Help? . . . . p. 32						
Write a Caption . . . . p. 34						
Pronunciation Guide	✗	✗	✗	✗	✗	✗
What Is a Pronunciation Guide? . . . . p. 35						
Say What? . . . . p. 36						
Bullets		✗	✗	✗	✗	✗
Text Bullets . . . . p. 37						
Reading Bullets . . . . p. 38						
All about Me in Bullets . . . . p. 39						
Using Bullets to Summarize . . . . p. 40						
Sidebars		✗	✗	✗	✗	✗
What Is a Sidebar? . . . . p. 41						
What Does a Sidebar Do? . . . . p. 42						
How Does It Relate? Part I . . . . p. 43						
How Does It Relate? Part II . . . . p. 45						
Readers' Theatre Script: What Are Print Features?						

Readers' Theatre Script Overview

Once your students have learned most or a good number of the text features in this chapter, you might consider accessing the CD for the readers' theatre script that corresponds to print features. The readers' theatre script can be used as a culminating activity or serve as an enrichment activity for students who excel at text features. You might even have a performance for parents at a family literacy evening or curriculum night.

Materials for Lessons

As you are teaching these text features, it is important to give special consideration to the types of text you use. It is worthwhile to spend the time to find interesting, well-written texts that contain good examples of the feature you are highlighting. We've included a limited bibliography of useful texts in **Appendix D: Suggested Resources for Teaching Text Features** (page 136). You should definitely supplement these with books from your classroom and school library. When the book fair is in town, take a moment to peruse the non-fiction selections. There are many great texts from which to choose. Please also remember that thinksheet lesson companions can be found on the CD.

Print Feature Lesson Definitions and Introductions

Titles, headings, and subheadings. Titles are arguably the most important feature of a text. Located on the cover or before the main body of text, titles briefly tell the reader what the passage is about. Headings and subheads further subdivide longer texts into digestible pieces within the topic. If asked to predict, a child can look to the title for guidance. If asked to summarize, a student in doubt can look back at the title to jog his memory. Even though it seems obvious to adult readers that the title tells what a text is about, many students fail to read or process this useful feature. Many teachers will tell you they teach about titles every time they read aloud or do guided reading with students. It seems this "teachable moment" approach isn't enough for most children. They need direct and consistent instruction in reading, using, and writing titles to ensure they use what they know when reading.

Bold print and italics. Students are aware of print at a very early age. They begin to notice when print is darker or when the font is italicized, but they may not understand why the print has been changed by the author. These lessons will help readers pay attention to print differences.

Captions. Captions are small sections of text that accompany graphic features and explain what is being shown. While a picture may be worth a thousand words, a picture and caption are worth more. Students who don't know the importance of captions are stuck using their imaginations to figure out what they are seeing when they look at non-fiction text features. It is really important to teach students not only to read captions, but also to include them in their own writing. A simple, "Can you write a caption for me here?" when a child shares an illustration can begin to get her in the habit.

Pronunciation guides. Pronunciation guides are phonetic spellings of new, difficult, and/or polysyllabic words right in the text. These follow the correctly spelled word and are set apart by parentheses. They are broken into syllables, with the emphasized syllable usually in all capital letters to help guide the reader. Knowing how to pronounce a word might help a child realize he has heard it before, fostering a connection to background knowledge. It will also allow students to read and say new words correctly. Teaching students what pronunciation guides are for and how to read them shouldn't take too much time as it relates nicely to word study activities you do in class. Pronouncing words correctly is important because it adds another layer of understanding to what is being read.

Bullets. Bullets are a writer's tool used to summarize and highlight important information. Knowing how and why to read bullets allows readers to quickly find and remember what is essential to the main idea. Knowing how to write bullets allows readers to reflect on what information they most want readers to understand and remember.

Sidebars. Aside from tables, sidebars may be the most neglected of all text features. Students who excitedly read pictures and captions will breeze right over a text box. A sidebar is a section of text set apart from the main body of writing. It is usually surrounded by a box or a different background color. Sidebars usually discuss a topic from the main body of text in more detail. We've seen sidebars with mini-biographies, how-tos, or elaborated details about an object in the text. Sometimes they include primary source documents or a poem related to the text. Whatever the content, it is important to read sidebars in order to get the full breadth of information about the main topic. Sidebars can be read before the main body of text or after, but usually should be read around the same time as the section they are related to.

Purpose

To help students determine which chapter titles are on the same topic and which chapter titles could be in the same book.

Prerequisite Skills

Students must understand that the title tells what the book is about and that the chapter titles are all subtopics of the main idea. Students must know how to do a dichotomous sort.

Materials

Thinksheet 2.2: Chapter Title Sort Cards cut apart and mounted on paper, if desired; *Thinksheet 2.1: Give Your Book a Title*

Directions

1. Review the idea that the title tells what the book is about. Show students the book title from your set of cards. Ask students to predict what types of information might be in a book with this title.
2. Tell students, "Longer books are broken into chapters, and each chapter is a small part of the main topic. These chapters have titles to help the reader find more specific information. For example, a book about tigers might have a chapter on types of tigers, another chapter on what tigers eat, and another chapter on where tigers live." This is a good time to pull out some age-appropriate examples from your classroom or school library.
3. Have students read through the chapter titles in the set. Ask them to sort the chapter titles into two piles: one with chapter titles that would be in this book, and one with chapter titles that would not be in this book.
4. Have them complete the first half of *Thinksheet 2.1: Give Your Book a Title* by filling in the book title and the appropriate chapter titles.
5. Ask students to write the rest of the chapter titles in the box provided on the thinksheet. Together, look at the leftover chapter titles and discuss what topic they fall under. Have students come up with a title for a book that these chapter titles would belong to. Have them write the book title in the line at the bottom of the box, and then have them share out loud. Discuss with students why they chose certain titles.

Modifications (for younger, less-able, or LEP students)

- Include pictures with each chapter title.
- Instead of using the thinksheet, use a large sheet of paper folded in half as a workmat
- Do this lesson as a whole group and scribe for students.

Assessment Options

As students gain confidence in their ability to categorize chapter titles, they can complete the work independently. At this point, it would also be appropriate to have students complete this assignment for a grade.

Technology

Use a document camera to show age-appropriate books with chapter titles. Have students use the interactive whiteboard to drag chapter titles into the correct space on the chart. Have them write in the book title and chapter titles.

Purpose

To help students understand that books are organized into chapters, which are subtopics of the main topic, and to reinforce that chapters, like books, have titles that tell what they are about. Students will also learn how authors organize chapters to help the reader best understand the topic.

Prerequisite Skills

Students must understand that the title of a book tells what the book is about and that the chapter titles are all subtopics of the main idea. Students must know how to do a dichotomous sort.

Materials

Thinksheet 2.2: Chapter Title Sort Cards—one complete set and enough sets of the chapter titles that don't belong to the book title for each pair of students to share one set

Directions

1. In a whole group, lead a sort of one set of chapter title cards, sorting them into two piles—one pile of chapter titles that go with the book title and one stack of chapter titles that do not go with the book title.
2. Explain to students that authors organize chapters to help the reader best understand the book topic. Point out the title of the book from the sort you just did and ask students to brainstorm what type of information might be in this book (knowing the chapter titles should help here).
3. Display the chapter titles and ask students what chapter topics might be the first ones in the book. Continue with the other chapter titles, making sure to elicit discussion among students about why they think certain topics go where. Remember, there is more than one right answer here, and the focus is on thinking about how non-fiction books are organized to help reveal information in a comprehensible way.
4. After the group lesson, have students break into pairs and then give them sets of the other chapter titles from the sort. Have them discuss and decide what the title of a book with those chapter titles would be and how these chapters could be organized.
5. Have pairs share out loud with the class and justify their choices.

Modifications (for younger, less-able, or LEP students)

- Use copies of actual pages from non-fiction trade books with the chapter titles on them.
- Do this activity one on one or in small groups instead of as a whole class.

Assessment Options

Conduct a performance assessment by having a student sort the chapter titles and put them in order. Students can then explain why they chose to order the chapters as they did.

Technology

A document camera could be used to model the students sorting and putting the chapter titles in order.

Purpose

To help students understand that chapter titles are all subtopics of a book title, and to help them understand how a table of contents is constructed based on key concepts. Note: Chapter 5 offers more activities involving table of contents.

Prerequisite Skills

Students must understand that the title of a book tells what the book is about and that the chapter titles are all subtopics of the main idea. Students must also know how to do a dichotomous sort.

Materials

Thinksheet 2.2: Chapter Title Sort Cards; Thinksheet 2.3: Create a Cover

Directions

1. Using one set of *Chapter Title Sort Cards (Thinksheet 2.2)* per pair, have students sort chapter titles into two different piles: one that has titles that fit with the provided book title and one that has titles that do not.
2. Have them set aside the chapter titles that fit with the book title and work only with the pile that has the chapter titles that do not fit with the book title.
3. Have partners discuss possible titles for a book with those chapter titles. Have them choose a title and write it in the appropriate space on the cover side of the *Thinksheet 2.3: Create a Cover*. It is okay if each of the students chooses a different title—the important thing is that they can justify their choices.
4. Have students discuss with partners what order they think the chapter titles should go in and then record the titles in the appropriate lines on the "Table of Contents" side of *Thinksheet 2.3: Create a Cover*.
5. Have students illustrate the covers of their books and then share out with the class.

Modifications (for younger, less-able, or LEP students)

- Can be done as a whole-group or small-group lesson so the teacher can step in more, if needed. It is okay for the teacher to read the titles aloud for nonreaders.
- Images related to the title and chapter titles could be used to improve comprehension.

Assessment Options

After students become more proficient with this structure and the concepts presented, grade this product.

Technology

Have students model sorting the cards. Once students have sorted, pull up the interactive Thinksheet 2.3 on an interactive whiteboard or on individual student computers. Fill in the book and chapter titles. Print, and have students illustrate the cover.

Directions:
1) Read your chapter title cards and think about what type of book these chapters would be in.
2) Decide on a title for your book and write it on the book cover, next to the word *Title*.
3) Decide which order the chapter titles might be in this book. Write the chapter titles in this order in the table of contents.
4) Draw a picture on your cover.

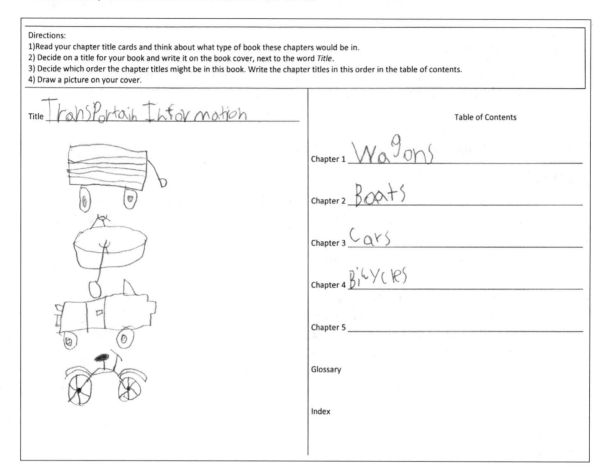

Title TransPortain Information

Table of Contents

Chapter 1 Wagons

Chapter 2 Boats

Chapter 3 Cars

Chapter 4 Bicycles

Chapter 5

Glossary

Index

Purpose

To help students understand that headings group a smaller section of text and explain what that section is about, and to use headings to find information in the text.

Prerequisite Skills

Students must understand that books are organized into chapters and chapters are subtopics of the main idea.

Materials

An example of a text with a title or chapter titles, and headings (science and social studies texts, as well as student periodicals such as *Weekly Reader* or *Time for Kids*, which usually have headings, can be used)

Directions

1. Tell students they will be learning about another important text feature: Headings and subheadings. Explain that headings are like chapter titles in that they tell what a section of text is about. The difference is that they describe a shorter section of text, from one paragraph to many, but they do not describe multiple pages. Headings are often found in science or social studies books, or in student magazines. Headings are usually written in a different color. They are in a smaller font than the title or chapter title but bigger than the main body of text. Tell students they can predict what a section of text will be about by reading the headings. They can also easily find information by looking at the headings to figure out where it might be located.

2. It is best to use an authentic piece of text for this lesson, but if you do not have access to textbooks or periodicals with headings, you can use the piece below (also found in Thinksheet 2.4 on the CD). Ask students to tell you what the title of the piece is. Next, ask them what the headings in this text are. As students list headings, jot them down on the board in the order they appear. Next, ask students if they can figure out what the text is about simply by reading the headings in order.

Help! Animals Need to Be Rescued
By Nicki Clausen-Grace

Millions of Lonely Pets

Every year, millions of pets are locked in kennels without anyone to love them because they have been abandoned by their owners. These cats and dogs usually haven't done anything wrong; their owners just don't want them any more. Sometimes the owners have died or lost a job, so they can't afford to care for their pets.

Where Are These Lonely Pets?

The luckiest of these pets are kept in shelters that help look for new owners. The less lucky animals get picked up by the county where they are put to sleep if no one claims them. All of these places feed the animals while they are in their care. They just don't have the time or money to play with them.

What You Can Do to Help

One way you can help is by never buying a puppy from a store. Instead, visit a shelter and adopt a lonely pet. Another way you can help is by making sure you can care for your pet for his whole life. Many shelters accept donations of money or food. Some even allow people to volunteer to clean crates, feed the animals, or take the dogs for walks. Everyone should do what he or she can to take care of these lonely pets.

---

3. Ask students to tell you the name of the heading under which they would expect to find information about how you can help the pets and where the pets are housed.
4. Either read the text aloud or have students silently read it to confirm or revise their predictions of what the text was about and where the information was located.
5. Ask students how headings help them predict and find information.

Modifications (for younger, less-able, or LEP students)

- Only do this lesson if your students are encountering texts with headings, as few texts for emergent readers include headings.
- If the provided text is not developmentally appropriate, use the texts from your classroom or school library.

Assessment Options

Notice if students can apply the prediction skills gained as they read texts with headings.

Technology

Display text on the projector or document camera.

Purpose

To have students notice, identify, and understand why an author uses bold and/or italicized print.

Prerequisite Skills

Students should know some sight words. Extension requires them to be able to write and read their name.

Materials

Interactive whiteboard (IWB), whiteboard, or computer

Directions

1. Write your name by hand on whiteboard. Type your name in Word or another program using three different styles. You will want to use a large font size so students can see the differences in the three print styles. Your name should be typed with a normal font, **bolded**, and then *italicized.* These could be pre-printed ahead of time or projected.

2. Ask students, "What do you notice about my name? How are they alike and how are they different?" If needed, explain that bold words are words written in a dark and thick print within the main body of text. Write the word BOLD, in bold, next to your typed name in bold print. Then, tell students, "Bold words in a book are usually defined in the glossary." Explain that italicized print is a font slanted to the right in the main body of text. Write the word *ITALICS, in italics,* next to the style of your name that was typed in italics.

3. Ask students, "Why would you use one of these writing styles over another?" (Point to each style, bold and *italics,* as you pose this question.)

4. If students do not answer correctly, say authors usually use bold print (point to or display an example) to tell readers that a word is important. Tell them that this helps readers understand what they are reading. While pointing to italics, tell students, "Authors use italics to tell you a word is important or to signal that you should emphasize this word when reading aloud."

5. Show some examples of regular font, bold, and italics. Use familiar sight words for this part of the activity. For example you might show the following:

Cat   **Cat**   *Cat*

6. Ask students to tell you which is bolded, normal print, and italicized. Have students label each word by the style. Repeat this with several words as necessary.

7. Review with students bold and *italic* print differences and why an author would use them.

8. Extension activity: Have students type their names in regular, bold, and *italics* font at computer stations. Have students label their name as normal, bold, and italic print. Because students may need assistance with typing and using the tools of the computer program you have, this may be a good activity to assign a volunteer to oversee.

Modifications (for younger, less-able, or LEP students)

Add pictures to go along with the words you use in the lesson and any follow-up activities. For example, you could have a picture of a cat next to the word cat used in this lesson.

Assessment Options

Observation will be critical in this lesson. Supply each student with a sheet of paper to label for step 5, and check for understanding. You could do step 5 as a clicker response on an interactive whiteboard.

Technology

See assessment options included in lesson step #7.

Note: This can be broken into two lessons—Part I (steps 1–5) and Part II (steps 6–7).

Purpose

To have students identify bold and italic print, and determine why the author used it in a text.

Prerequisite Skills

Students should be able to identify bold and italic print and have some basic awareness that the author uses these types of print to signal important vocabulary (words).

Materials

Interactive whiteboard or chart paper, pre-selected text with bold and italic print, *Thinksheet 2.5: Bold and Italic Word Detective-see below*; magnifying glass (optional)

Bold and *Italic* Word Detectives Thinksheet

Name of Text _____

Word	Page # Found	Is it Bold or *Italic*??	Why I think the author used bold or *italicized* print ...
1.			
2.			
3.			
4.			
5.			

Directions

1. Write the terms *bold* and *italics* on an interactive whiteboard or class chart. Review the differences between bold and italic print. If needed, explain that bolded words are words written in a dark and thick print within the main body of text. Show an example. If appropriate, add that bolded words are usually defined in the glossary. Then, explain that italicized print is a font slanted to the right and also in the main part of the text. Show an example.
2. Review the importance of bold and italic print. Tell students that authors usually use bold print (point to an example) and italic print (point to an example) to tell readers that this word is important or to signal the readers to emphasize the word while reading."
3. Tell students that today they will be detectives, explaining what a detective is if students don't know. Partner students and tell them they will hunt for bolded or italicized words. Have them use the *Bold and Italic Word Detective* thinksheet to record each word they found and the page they found it on. The lesson will be more productive if students share the same pages of a common text (we recommend two pages of pre-selected text). You could also differentiate this lesson further by placing students in guided-reading groups and then conduct the rest of this lesson in small groups.

4. Before letting students work on their own, you will want to show them how to complete the first part of the *Bold and Italic Word Detective* thinksheet (columns 1–3; older students will be able to move to column 4 if you model at this point). Open a shared text with bold or italicized print. Ask students to help you be a detective and find a bold or italicized word. When they located a bold or italic word, complete the first part of the thinksheet so students can see what they will need to do. Write the word in the first column. Ask, "What page is the word on?" Again you can elicit student responses here. Then, in the second column, put the page number where you found the word. Think aloud and ask, "Is this a bold or italic word?" so that students can see what they should be thinking about as they complete the exercise. You can have students offer ideas if you wish. In the third column write whether it is bold or italic. Tell them they will complete the fourth column with you in small or as a whole group, unless you feel the students are developmentally ready to complete the last column. If this is true look at step 6 for further guidance.

5. Have students work in pairs to find bold and italic print, and have them complete the first three columns of their thinksheet. You might want to have them put a sticky note over the last column so they do not jump ahead.

6. When students have completed step 5, bring them together either as a group, if you used a shared text, or as small guided-reading groups. Ask students to share a bold or italicized word they found. Using an enlarged copy of the thinksheet, begin filling in the chart using what the students have already completed in step 5. Continue until you have all of the bold and italic words added onto the thinksheet. Tell them, "We now need to figure out why the author used bold or italics for these words. Let's read this section of text (with the first bold or italic word) to figure out why the author chose this word." Read aloud and then ask, "Why do you think the author made this word bold (or italic)?" Guide their responses if needed, and then complete the last column of the thinksheet.

7. Continue until all words are discussed. Review why an author would bold or italicize a word. Ask students, "Why do you think I taught you about bold and italic print?" If needed, tell them you expect them to notice bold and italic print and that you want them to think about why the author chose to emphasize certain words.

Modifications (for younger, less-able, or LEP students)

- See steps 3 and 4 for modifications.
- You can pair students up strategically.

Assessment Options

Observation and *Thinksheet 2.5: Bold and Italic Word Detective.*

Technology

Steps 1–4, as well as steps 6–7, could be done on an interactive whiteboard.

Purpose

To help students identify captions, and to help them understand that captions describe a graphic feature related to the main body of text.

Prerequisite Skills

Students must know the difference between a text feature and the main body of text. They must also be somewhat familiar with what maps and pictures look like, and they must know how to match cards that go together.

Materials

Student textbooks or non-fiction trade books that open to a two-page spread with both main body of text and at least one text feature with a caption; *Thinksheet 2.6: Caption Match Sorting Cards*

Directions

1. Ask students to tell you what the main body of text is and to point to it in their textbooks. Observe students as they do this to check for understanding.
2. Ask students to point to a text feature in the text. Observe students to be sure they know the difference between the main body of text and a text feature.
3. Tell students, "Today you will be learning about a very important text feature— the caption. Captions explain other graphic features such as pictures, photos, maps, and diagrams. Not all of these graphic features always have a caption, but they often do."
4. Show the image below (also found in the Chapter 2 folder on the CD. Ask students what this is a picture of. They will probably not be able to give an accurate answer.

5. Next, add the caption to the image or read the caption aloud "flamingo feather close-up: This close up of a flamingo's tail feather shows how pink these birds can become from eating pink shrimp.". Ask students to tell you what the image shows now (based on the caption). Ask them what the main body of text might be about if this were a text feature on a page. Examples of answers would include: what animals eat, birds, flamingos, etc.
6. Tell students that it is important to read the captions because without doing so, they might get the wrong idea about what they are seeing or what they will read about. Graphic images should help you learn more about the main body of text, but they can't do so if you don't really know what you are looking at.
7. Ask students to point out some captions in their text. As they share, ask them what each caption explains. Example answers are: pictures, maps, diagrams, graphs, etc.
8. Tell students that they are going to practice matching captions with the graphic features they go with. Hand out *Thinksheet 2.6: Caption Match Sorting Cards*, and go over the directions.
9. After students complete the sort, go over their answers and have them explain their thinking.
10. Ask students to think about all these pictures and captions, and have them predict what the main body of text these features go with might be about.

Modifications (for younger, less-able, or LEP students)

- Break this into two lessons, with the sort being completed the next day.
- Read aloud and do the sort together as a class.

Assessment Options

Observe who can correctly match graphic features to captions.

Technology

Use a document camera to show the image of the flamingo feather. You can also use an interactive whiteboard to show the image, post match cards (2.5), and complete using an e-pen.

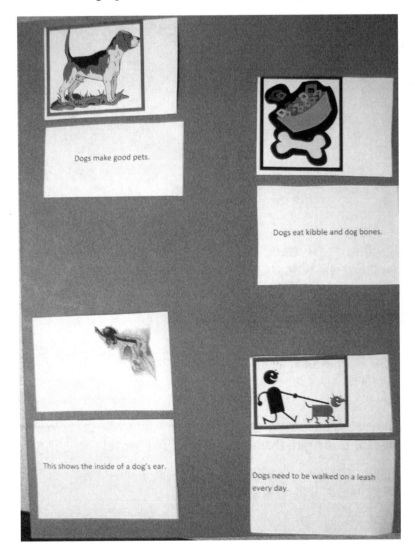

Purpose

To help students see how captions, along with the graphic features, explain and relate to the main body of text.

Prerequisite Skills

Students must know the difference between a text feature and the main body of text, and they must know how to match cards. Students must also be able to tell what captions are, and how they are used.

Materials

Thinksheet 2.7: Where Does It Fit?; T-chart made of construction paper for each pair of students that should look like this:

Animals of the Forest	Our Clothes

Directions

1. Ask students to tell you what captions are and how they are used. They should be able to tell you that captions are small pieces of text that explain a graphic feature such as a picture, map, or diagram.
2. Ask students why authors use captions with graphic features. They should be able to tell you that captions, and the features they explain, help show a detail from the main body of text. Ask students if you can put a feature on any topic in any text. Again, they should be able to tell you that graphic features and their captions further explain only the main body of the text.
3. Hand out *Thinksheet 2.7: Where Does It Fit?* and go over the directions.
4. Have students work in pairs to determine which picture and caption goes with which main idea. Discuss student's answers.

Modifications (for younger, less-able, or LEP students)

- Read aloud and complete the thinksheet as a class or small group.
- Make the thinksheet into sorting cards instead.

Assessment Options

Score individually completed thinksheets to see if students can correctly match features with the main topic.

Technology

Use an interactive whiteboard to show and complete the thinksheet using an e-pen.

Purpose

To help students understand that graphic images, along with their captions, help explain the main body of text.

Prerequisite Skills

Students must have knowledge of captions and the fact that they relate to the main body of text, and they must also have completed *Thinksheet 2.7: Where Does It Fit?*

Materials

Graphic feature/caption cards; chart paper with the following T-chart drawn on it:

Animals of the Forest	Our Clothes

Directions

1. Hand back the completed *Thinksheet 2.7: Where Does It Fit?* from the previous lesson. Ask students to help you complete the chart by placing the various feature/caption cards under the correct title. Leave room for writing beside or below each card (see example).

Animals of the Forest	Our Clothes
How it helps …	How it helps …

2. After the cards are in place, explain that features and captions are there to help the reader fully understand the main body of text. Choose one of the titles and, as a class, analyze each feature and caption to decide how they help the reader understand the topic of this text. Write how it helps next to each feature.
3. After you have discussed all of the features and captions, ask students, "Do you think these features help you understand _____ (insert the title of the book)? How?"

Modifications (for younger, less-able, or LEP students)

- Brainstorm background knowledge about the title you choose to discuss—select a topic students are familiar with.
- Work one-on-one or in a small group.

Assessment Options

Observe to see who participates meaningfully.

Technology

Use a document camera to show the T-chart on your screen. Show and complete the T-chart on your interactive whiteboard.

Purpose

To help students apply their knowledge of captions to writing.

Prerequisite Skills

Students must have knowledge of captions and know that captions relate to the main body of text.

Materials

Thinksheet 2.8: Write a Caption

Directions

1. Ask students to tell you what captions are and what they do. They should be able to tell you that captions are small pieces of text that explain a graphic feature such as a picture, map, or diagram and that graphic features and captions help you learn more about the main idea of a text.
2. Tell students that today they will be writing captions for features that go with a piece of text. They will be writing about something they know well—school.
3. Share the text, "School," from *Thinksheet 2.8*. Ask students to restate what the text is about.
4. Discuss each graphic feature below the text, ensuring each student knows what is being depicted.
5. Instruct students to write captions below each graphic feature. Remind them that these captions should explain the feature and go into more detail about something in the text.
6. Have students share their captions.

Modifications (for younger, less-able, or LEP students)

- Write the captions as a class, read back chorally.
- Work one-on-one or in a small group.

Assessment Options

Check to ensure captions relate to the graphic features and the main body of text.

Technology

Use a document camera or an interactive whiteboard to display and complete the thinksheet.

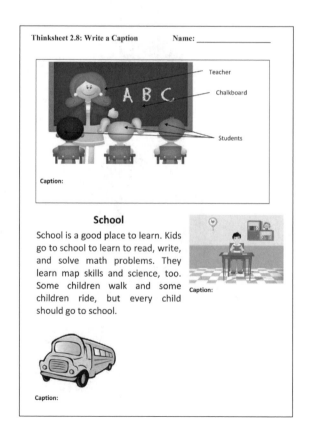

Thinksheet 2.8: Write a Caption   Name: _____

Teacher

Chalkboard

Students

Caption:

School

School is a good place to learn. Kids go to school to learn to read, write, and solve math problems. They learn map skills and science, too. Some children walk and some children ride, but every child should go to school.

Caption:

Caption:

Purpose

To help students understand why pronunciation guides are included in texts and how to use them.

Prerequisite Skills

Students must know how to read common phonetic groupings of letters and know what syllables are.

Materials

Examples from student periodicals like *Weekly Reader,* content-area texts, or the text below

Directions

1. Tell students that today they are going to learn about an important text feature that helps them sound like they know what they are talking about. It is called a pronunciation guide, and it helps readers say important, new, or difficult words correctly.

2. Ask students why it is important to read words correctly. They might say so other people know what you mean or so you understand what you are reading. Share an example of a time you read a word incorrectly and it changed the meaning. You can say, "One time I was opening a birthday present from my brother. Trying to act happy as soon as I could see the writing, I excitedly called out 'SCRAPES! I love SCRAPES!' It was actually a *SCRAP* book (which sounds a lot more fun that *scrapes*, doesn't it?)." Point out that if you knew how to pronounce the word, you would have realized you knew what the gift actually was. Sometimes, pronunciation guides help us realize we actually know an unfamiliar-looking word.

3. Tell students that there are also times when you see an unfamiliar word and you haven't ever heard it. The pronunciation guide helps you pronounce the word correctly the very first time.

4. Use one of your samples or the example below:

   Marine (MUH-reen) animals live in the ocean. Dolphins, whales, otters, and sharks are all marine animals. There are many different species (SPEE-seez) living in the ocean.

5. Model reading the excerpt, pointing to the pronunciation guides as you read them. Tell students to notice how the *MUH* in *marine* is emphasized. Read it the other way (muh-REEN) to help them hear the difference between emphasizing the first and second syllable. Tell them sometimes the emphasized syllable is all in capital letters and sometimes it is in bold print. Ask if any of the students have heard the words *marine* and *species* before. Ask how the pronunciation guide would help them read this excerpt.

6. Remind students that pronunciation guides help us correctly say the important, new, or confusing words in a text.

Modifications (for younger, less-able, or LEP students)

- Use a lower-level text for the example.
- Model with pronunciation guides of single-syllable words.

Assessment Options

Pay attention to whether or not students understand how to emphasize the correct syllable. If they have trouble, spend more time on this in the follow-up lesson.

Technology

Use an online periodical such as *Weekly Reader* or *Time for Kids* to show examples of pronunciation guides. Point out that often online texts have a button to click to have the word read aloud.

Purpose

To help students read words that are phonetically represented.

Prerequisite Skills

Students must know how to read common phonetic groupings of letters and what syllables are. They should have been introduced to the concept of emphasizing certain syllables. Students should also be able to find words in a children's dictionary.

Materials

Student dictionaries (preferably the *Scholastic Children's Dictionary*, but any will do)—at least one per pair of students

Directions

1. Ask students to tell you what pronunciation guides are. They should be able to tell you that pronunciation guides are in the main body of text and they help readers say important, new, or difficult words correctly. They should remember that words are broken into syllables, written the way they sound, and that the emphasized syllable is the one written all in capital letters or bold print. If they have forgotten any of these key components, review with them.

2. Tell them that today they will practice reading words that are written the way the pronunciation guide shows them. Since dictionaries also write words in this manner, you will be using a dictionary.

3. Write the word *arena* on the board and tell students to find it in the dictionary. Once students have located the word, write it on the board the way it is represented in the pronunciation guide (uh-ree-nuh) or (uh-REE-nuh). Have students practice reading this word using the pronunciation guide. Model how to emphasize the second syllable.

4. Continue with other polysyllabic words (a few suggestions include chassis, depot, fasten, machete, scenario).

5. Encourage your students to find a word new to them and share both how it is written and how to read it. Have students take turns writing their words in pronunciation guide form on a piece of chart paper as they share. Display the chart paper to serve as a reminder.

Modifications (for younger, less-able, or LEP students)

Do the entire lesson as a teacher-guided activity using a shared text.

Assessment Options

Listen as students read their words from the dictionary to see if they are reading them correctly. If not, step in to guide them.

Technology

Display the dictionary pages on the projector.

Purpose

To help students identify bulleted text.

Prerequisite Skills

Students must have some knowledge of what it means to summarize.

Materials

Thinksheet 2.9: Text Bullets—either one per pair or shown on a whiteboard with a projection device

Directions

1. Tell students, "Today we will be learning about a special kind of text feature: bullets. Bullets are key points in a piece of text. They are usually set apart by being lined up on a wider indent than regular text and each point has a dot or small icon in front of it. Writers use bullets to summarize something important."

2. Share the text example at the top of *Thinksheet 2.9: Text Bullets*. Tell students, "The author may have chosen to write the information in another form." Share the bulleted example on the thinksheet and ask students, "Which form was easier to read and remember?" Explain, "Sometimes authors choose to put important information in bulleted form because they want it to be easier to read and remember."

3. Show the bottom half of the thinksheet, and ask students, "Which text is in bullet form?"

4. Have them read each set of bullets and tell what they learned.

Modifications (for younger, less-able, or LEP students)

- Read all of the text for students.
- Work-one-on one or in a small group.

Assessment Options

Observe to ensure students can visually differentiate between bulleted and other types of text.

Technology

Use a document camera or an interactive whiteboard to display *Thinksheet 2.9*.

Purpose

To help students read bullets to gain information.

Prerequisite Skills

Students must be able to identify bulleted text and know that it summarizes key points. Students must also understand that titles tell what a text is about.

Materials

Thinksheet 2.10: Reading Bullets—either one per pair or shown on a whiteboard with a projection device

Directions

1. Ask students, "What are bullets? What do they look like and what they are used for?" They should be able to tell you that bullets are key points in a piece of text that are usually set apart by being lined up on a narrower indent than regular text. Each point has a dot or small icon in front of it. And, writers use bullets to summarize something important.

2. Tell students, "Today we will be reading bullets to learn how authors organize and present information to readers." Hand out or display *Thinksheet 2.10: Reading Bullets*. Read aloud or ask students to read the first set of bullets. Have them either write or share what they learned from reading the bullets. They should say something like, "Horses need water, food, and exercise." Ask, "What might the topic for the main body of text be if these bullets were included?" Possible answers include, "Horses, What Horses Need, Horses as Pets, etc."

3. Continue with the other examples, allowing students to read and work independently as soon as they are ready.

Modifications (for younger, less-able, or LEP students)

- Read all text to students.
- Work one-on-one or in a small group.

Assessment Options

Observe to see if students are able to glean information from bullets. If not, model reading and retelling bullets for them. Also watch to see if they are able to come up with a reasonable title for a related text. If not, consider re-teaching some of the title lessons.

Technology

Use a document camera or an interactive whiteboard to display the thinksheet, retellings, and titles.

Reading Bullets   Name Sarah

Directions: Read each set of bullets. On the line underneath, write what you learned from reading the bullets. On the next line, write a possible title for a book you might find these bullets in.

1) Horses need:

- Water
- Food
- Shoes
- Exercise

What I learned: I learned that horses needs exercise, shoes, food and water.

These bullets might be in a book with this title: What horses need to survive

2) Girls wear:

- Shirts
- Shorts
- Pants
- Skirts
- Dresses

What I learned: I learned that girls wear lots of clothes like shirts, shorts, pants, skirts and dresses.

These bullets might be in a book with this title: What Girls Wear

1) If you want to play baseball you must have:

- A ball
- A bat
- Bases
- Gloves
- Other players

What I learned: I learned that if you want to play baseball you must have alot of stuff like a ball, a bat, bases, gloves and of course other players.

These bullets might be in a book with this title: What you need to play Baseball other players.

Purpose

To begin writing bullets to summarize key points.

Prerequisite Skills

Students must understand both the purpose and proper use of bullets.

Materials

Thinksheet 2.11: All about Me in Bullets; pencils or crayons

Directions

1. Ask students, "What are bullets used for?" They should be able to tell you that bullets are key points in a piece of text that are usually set apart by being lined up on a narrower indent than regular text. Each point has a dot or small icon in front of it. And, writers use bullets to summarize something important.
2. Tell students, "Today you will be writing bullets to describe yourself." Show an example of how you might write bullets to describe yourself. You might write something like:

All about Me

My name is Mrs. Grace. I am a 44-year-old teacher. I have:

- Blue eyes
- Blond hair
- Freckles

3. Draw a picture or have a photograph to go with the bullets.
4. Give students the thinksheet (2.11). Have them write two sentences introducing themselves, then have them list something about themselves in bulleted form. They might bullet their hobbies, special talents, looks, names of siblings, names of pets, places they have lived, etc.
5. Give students some time to write while you circulate and help.
6. Have students draw a picture of themselves to go with the bullets they listed (on *Thinksheet 2.11*).
7. After students write, have them share with each other. As they share, have the other students tell what they learned from the bullets.

Modifications (for younger, less-able, or LEP students)

Provide a word bank using words that students request.

Assessment Options

Assess thinksheets to make sure students are putting things that go together in their bulleted lists.

Technology

Use a document camera or interactive whiteboard to display.

Purpose

To help students summarize using bullets.

Prerequisite Skills

Students must be able to identify bulleted text and know it summarizes key points. Students must also be familiar with summarizing, although they do not need to have mastered the skill.

Materials

Thinksheet 2.12: Using Bullets to Summarize

Directions

1. Ask students, "What are bullets used for?" They should be able to tell you that writers use bullets to summarize something important.
2. Hand out *Thinksheet 2.12* and tell students they will be rewriting the text using bullets.
3. Model the first example with students, and then have them complete the rest on their own. Choose a student or two to write their bullets on the board.

Modifications (for younger, less-able, or LEP students)

- Read the text aloud.
- Complete the activity as a class, or have students work with partners.

Assessment Options

Assess whether or not students were able to create bullets that are indented, aligned, have dots or icons in front, and accurately distill the section of text they are rewriting.

Technology

Use a document camera or interactive whiteboard to display.

Using Bullets to Summarize   Name ___Trinity___

Directions: Read each paragraph. After each, choose one part to summarize using bullets. Remember that the bullets all need to be about the same topic.

1) Cooking
Cooking is a great way to have fun and make treats for your family and friends. You can make cookies. You can make a cake. You can even make hamburgers. The one thing you cannot make is the tools you need for cooking. You need bowls. You need spoons. You need pans. You need measuring cups. If you have all the tools and ingredients, you can cook food that tastes great. Write the stem and bullets here

Tools we need to cook :
- bowls
- spoons
- pans
- measuring cups

2) Football
Many children want to play football when they grow up. Not many people get to have this job though. If you want to be a professional football player you need to be big. You need to be strong. You need to have talent. You also need to be hard-working and lucky. It is probably a good idea to have another job in mind in case you don't end up playing football. Write the stem and bullets here
To be a professional football player you need
- to be big
- to be strong
- to have talent
- hard working
- to be lucky

3) Matter
Everything that takes up space and has mass is called **matter**. Candy is matter. Juice is matter. Even air is matter. There are three different forms of matter. The first is **solid**. The second is **liquid**. The last is **gas**. Even you are made of matter.
Write the stem and bullets here
There are 3 forms of matter :
- solid
- liquid
- gas

Purpose

To help students identify sidebars and their purpose.

Prerequisite Skills

Students must know what the main body of text and a text feature are.

Materials

Examples of non-fiction texts that have sidebars, such as a science or social studies textbook, or trade books

Directions

1. Tell students that sidebars are text features that are set apart from the main body of text in a box or with a shaded background. There can be lots of different types of information in a sidebar, but it should always in some way be related to the main body of text.
2. Direct students to a page in your sample text that has both a main body of text and at least one sidebar. Have students run their hands over the main body of text and explain what this is. Next, have them point to a sidebar. Observe students to make sure everyone has found the sidebar.
3. Ask students to tell you how the sidebar looks different from the main body of text (it should have a different colored background or a box around it and is located at the top, side, or bottom of the page).
4. Ask students to find other examples of sidebars in their text. Monitor to ensure they can correctly identify this text feature and have students share out loud.

Modifications (for younger, less-able, or LEP students)

- Show several examples of sidebars.
- Model how to trace the main body of text and where to touch the sidebars.

Assessment Options

Observe to ensure students can correctly identify sidebars.

Technology

Use a document camera to show pages in a textbook or trade book.

Purpose

To help students identify sidebars and their purpose.

Prerequisite Skills

Students must know what the main body of text and a text feature are, what a sidebar looks like, and how to find the chapter title or heading for a section of text.

Materials

Examples of non-fiction texts that have sidebars, such as a science or social studies textbook, or a trade book; *Thinksheet 2.13: Which Sidebar Fits?*

Directions

1. Ask students to tell you what a sidebar looks like. They should say something like, "It has a different colored background or a box around it, and is found at the top, side, or bottom of the page."
2. Have students find a sidebar in their sample text. Ask them what the main body of text in that section is about. They don't have to read the main body of text; they can simply read the chapter title or section heading.
3. Either have a student read the sidebar aloud, or you can read to the students as they follow along. Ask them what the sidebar was about. Ask students how the sidebar relates to the main body of text. Tell students that sidebars relate to the main body of text, but that they also go into more detail by explaining a process, or how something is done. Tell students that sidebars may tell about a person who was important to the topic, such as an inventor who created something or a researcher who discovered something.
4. Hand out the *Thinksheet 2.13: Which Sidebar Fits?*, and explain the directions. You may want to do the first one with students.
5. Have students complete the thinksheet, and then discuss their answers.

Modifications (for younger, less-able, or LEP students)

Read aloud and complete the thinksheet together.

Assessment Options

The thinksheet can be graded, although there are not many items on it so it might be best to use it to help guide future lessons.

Technology

Use a document camera to show the main body of text and related sidebar. Use an interactive whiteboard to complete the thinksheet.

Purpose

To help students apply their knowledge of how sidebars relate to the main body of text.

Prerequisite Skills

Students must know what a sidebar is and how it relates to the main body of text. It is helpful if they have completed the first two lessons in this sequence.

Materials

Examples of non-fiction texts that have sidebars, such as a science or social studies textbook, or trade book; whiteboard or chart paper; "Pets" text (in lesson plan)

Directions

1. Ask students to tell you what a sidebar is and how it is used. They should tell you something like, "A sidebar has a different colored background or a box around it and is found at the top, side, or bottom of the page. It is used to give additional detailed information about the main body of text." Tell your students that today they will be reading a main body of text and coming up with ideas for sidebars that are related to the text but go into more detail.
2. Share the following text either on the whiteboard or chart paper. You can read it to or with students.

Pets

Do you have a pet? Pets are animals that people adopt and take care of. Many people think of a pet as a member of their family. They feed them every day and give them lots of love. Some pets are small, like hamsters, and some pets are big, like horses. Some pets are easy to take care of and some pets are harder to take care of. Some pets, such as cats, you can hold. Other pets, like a fish, can't be held. No matter what kind of pet you have, it needs to be cared for every day.

3. Ask students to discuss the main idea of this text. Make sure you come to an agreement as a class about the main idea. Some examples might be "pets," "pets need care," "different kinds of pets," etc. Write the main idea at the top of the board or chart paper. Label this "Main Idea."
4. Ask students to brainstorm details or more specific ideas that could be sidebars for this text. Make text boxes to write these in. Label this section, "Possible Sidebars." See example:

> **Main Idea:** Pets Need Care
>
> Sidebar Ideas:

5. As students generate ideas, ask them, "How does that relate to the main idea?" Some sidebar suggestions they may come up with include: "Taking Care of a Cat (or Dog, Guinea Pig, etc.)," "Horses (or Dogs, Cats, Gerbils, etc.) as Pets," "Pets You Can Snuggle."
6. When you feel students get the idea, ask them to tell you what sidebars are and how they are used.

Modifications (for younger, less-able, or LEP students)

- Before reading the text, have students brainstorm what they know about pets.
- Have pictures of the pets discussed in the text available as well as other types of pets they may bring up.

Assessment Options

Have students create their own list of possible sidebar ideas to go along with this topic. Assess their work to see if all ideas are related to the main idea.

Technology

Display the text or show pictures of the animals on a document camera. Create your simple chart on the interactive whiteboard and have students fill in their answers. Show photos of the animals discussed on the board.

Purpose

To help students apply their knowledge of how sidebars relate to the main body of text, and to allow students to write sidebars related to the main topic.

Prerequisite Skills

Students must know what a sidebar is and how it relates to the main body of text. They must have done the first "How Does It Relate?" lesson in order to effectively do this one.

Materials

Main body of text written on chart paper or the board ("Pets" text—see lesson plan); completed chart from the first "How Does It Relate? lesson; sidebar paper for each student (sidebar paper should be cut into a narrow rectangle or box and have a shaded/colored background or an outline around the box; you decide if your students do better with or without lines)

Directions

1. Ask students to tell you what a sidebar is and how it is used. They should say something like, "A sidebar has a different colored background or a box around it; is found at the top, side, or bottom of the page; and is used to give extra, more detailed information about the main body of text." Tell them they will be writing a sidebar to go with text from the last lesson.
2. Re-read the main body of text:

Pets

Do you have a pet? Pets are animals that people adopt and take care of. Many people think of a pet as a member of their family. They feed them every day and give them lots of love. Some pets are small, like hamsters, and some pets are big, like horses. Some pets are easy to take care of and some pets are harder to take care of. Some pets, such as cats, you can hold. Other pets, like a fish, can't be held. No matter what kind of pet you have, it needs to be cared for every day.

3. Review the sidebar ideas chart you made in class. Ask students to select one of the sidebar ideas to use as a topic for a sidebar they will write. It's okay if some students select the same topics.
4. Have students brainstorm ideas for their sidebar topics. They can do this with an elbow partner or, if possible, with students who chose the same topic to write about.
5. Have students write their sidebars on a piece of shaded or boxed paper. One to three sentences should be enough. You can decide if you want them to take this through stages of the writing process before publishing it on sidebar paper or if a rough draft will suffice to get the idea across.
6. Have students share their pieces and tape them around the main body of text, as they might be placed in a book.

Modifications (for younger, less-able, or LEP students)

Write a sidebar together as a class, use picture cards to help students brainstorm ideas, and create a word bank to assist with writing.

Assessment Options

Read sidebars to see if students wrote about a related topic in more depth.

Technology

Display the text, along with pictures of the animals, on a document camera. You can also show the chart from the first lesson, and animal photos, on an interactive whiteboard.

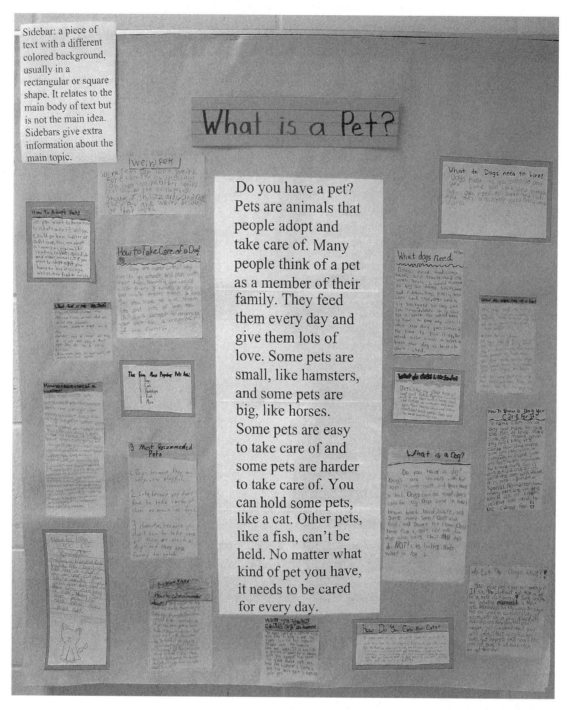

Sidebar: a piece of text with a different colored background, usually in a rectangular or square shape. It relates to the main body of text but is not the main idea. Sidebars give extra information about the main topic.

Chapter 3
Graphic Features Mini-lessons

Overview for Teaching Graphic Features

Sometimes a picture is truly worth more than a thousand words. Without the support of images, reading about something new or challenging is very difficult indeed. Readers rely on images to help them make sense of concepts and to visualize something.

Pictures, maps, diagrams, charts, and other graphic features are the most commonly encountered hallmark of quality non-fiction expository text. They are also the most frequently misinterpreted text feature. For example, students may fail to connect a map with the content of a text. Or, they might not read the titles of maps, graphs, diagrams, and cross-sections, therefore forfeiting the ability to contextualize the graphic. They often lack the background to understand what the author wanted them to see, think about, or understand when she decided to include a certain graphic.

Yet there is great potential in teaching children to read graphic features because they contain so much rich and accessible information. Students who take a moment to read and comprehend the images included with a piece of text will have much greater comprehension than those who just give the features a cursory glance.

The graphics features lessons are arranged in ascending order of difficulty, starting from the easiest. For teaching purposes, we have grouped some of the text features together. The table below lists the features taught in this chapter and the grade level(s) when these features should be mastered.

Figure 5: **Graphic Features End-of-grade-level Expectations and Lessons Related to Each Text Feature**

GRAPHIC FEATURES End-of-grade-level Expectations and Lessons Related to Each Text Feature	K	1	2	3	4	5
Photographs and Drawings	✗	✗	✗	✗	✗	✗
What Is a Picture? . . . . p. 51						
Pictures with Captions . . . . p. 52						
Which Picture? . . . . p. 53						
Insets	✗	✗	✗	✗	✗	✗
What Is an Inset? . . . . p. 54						
Set in What? . . . . p. 55						
Inset Hunt. . . . . p. 57						
Create an Inset . . . . p. 58						

Continued

GRAPHIC FEATURES End-of-grade-level Expectations and Lessons Related to Each Text Feature	K	1	2	3	4	5
Cross-sections/Cutaways			✗	✗	✗	✗
What's Inside? Part I . . . . p. 60						
What's Inside? Part II . . . . p. 62						
Cross-section Scavenger Hunt. . . . . p. 63						
Labeled Diagrams		✗	✗	✗	✗	✗
Using a Photograph or Labeled Diagram. . . . . p. 64						
Diagrams		✗	✗	✗	✗	✗
The Anatomy of a Diagram . . . . p. 66						
Introduction: How to Read a Diagram. . . . . p. 67						
Using a Diagram to Answer Questions . . . . p. 68						
What Is a Venn Diagram? . . . . p. 69						
Creating a Diagram. . . . . p. 70						
Maps		✗	✗	✗	✗	✗
What Is a Map? . . . . p. 72						
Anatomy of a Map: Parts of a Map . . . . p. 74						
Reviewing Map Parts and How to Read Maps . . . . p. 76						
Creating a Map. . . . . p. 77						
Timelines		✗	✗	✗	✗	✗
What Is a Timeline?. . . . . p. 79						
Reading a Timeline . . . . p. 80						
Creating a Classroom Timeline. . . . . p. 81						
Creating a Timeline with Children's Literature. . . . . . . p. 82						
Creating My Timeline. . . . . p. 84						
Graphs		✗	✗	✗	✗	✗
What Is a Graph?. . . . . p. 86						
The Anatomy of a Graph . . . . p. 87						
Reading a Graph . . . . p. 88						
Creating a Graph . . . . p. 89						
Charts/Tables			✗	✗	✗	✗
What Is a Table?. . . . . p. 91						
The Anatomy of a Table and Reading a Chart/Table . . . p. 93						
Creating a Table. . . . . p. 95						
Readers' Theatre Script: What Are Graphic Features?						

Readers' Theatre Script Overview

Once your students have learned most or a good number of the text features in this chapter, you might consider accessing the CD for the readers' theatre script that corresponds to print features. The readers' theatre script can be used as a culminating activity or serve as an enrichment activity for students who excel at text features. You might even have a performance for parents at a family literacy evening or curriculum night.

Materials for Lessons

As you are teaching these text features, it is important to give special consideration to the types of text you use. It is worthwhile to spend the time to find interesting, well-written texts that contain good examples of the feature you are highlighting. We've included a limited bibliography of useful texts in **Appendix D: Suggested Resources for Teaching Text Features** (page 136). You should definitely supplement these with books from your classroom and school library. When the book fair is in town, take a moment to peruse the non-fiction selections. There are many great texts from which to choose. Please also remember that thinksheet lesson companions can be found on the CD.

Graphic Feature Lesson Definitions and Introductions

Photographs and drawings (with or without captions). Developmentally, the concept of a picture can be taught to all school-aged children. A picture can either be a drawing or photograph. Drawing is usually a student's first attempt at writing. Additionally, most students have had their photograph taken and know someone who has a camera. Therefore, the use of pictures will be a concept they have some prior knowledge with. The lessons in this section include teaching the purpose of including pictures with text, the use of captions with pictures, and creating or choosing a picture (drawing or photograph) to go with text

Insets. Have you ever seen a picture taken from far away and wondered what the subject would look like close up? Insets show a close-up detail of a larger picture. It might show a horde of bees and then one up close or a mangrove forest with a close-up of the root tangle. Authors include insets in order to give readers a broader understanding of what is being shown on a couple of levels. Thinking about why an author might choose to include an inset is a good way to prepare students for creating their own to go along with their writing.

Cross-sections and cutaways. Cross-sections show the inside of something that has been cut completely through. These allow readers to see the inner workings of things that wouldn't usually be possible. Examples include cross-sections of the Earth, a flower, or a seed. Often, these are also labeled diagrams with labels pointing to the details readers should pay attention to. Since children are naturally curious about things they can't see, it makes sense that they would enjoy reading and creating cross-sections. Cutaways show the inside of something, but they show the outside of what is being illustrated, too. A cutaway has just a piece of the outside dissolved to show the inner workings. An example is a picture of a ship with most of the hull intact and a circle of the hull dissolved to show inside the ship. It is not cut in half.

Diagrams. Diagrams come in different sizes and shapes. Some have labels, and some do not. Diagrams often involve multiple pictures (and text), as they often explain steps or a process. Therefore, some diagrams require a reader to determine what order the pictures should be studied and then integrate this with the information in the text. Students must understand what is in the text and diagram, decide how the two are related, and then determine whether the information in the diagram is important to the text. Teaching children how to read and learn from diagrams can be challenging but is necessary as textbooks are increasingly using diagrams to explain important content. Furthermore, diagram reading and application is often tested on high-stakes assessments in the intermediate grades.

Maps. Maps are all around us. Children can learn about maps at a very young age. In fact, most children will have seen an adult use a map before they enter kindergarten. By first grade, students should be ready to use maps to assist with reading. Therefore, they need to know the parts of a map, such as the title, key or legend, and compass rose. By third grade, you might introduce various types of maps, such as geographical maps, weather maps, and political maps. Because the concept of mapmaking—the idea of real places being put on a flat surface with symbols—is so abstract, you might begin by creating a map of something familiar, such your classroom, the school, or the neighborhood.

Timelines. Timelines are a staple of social studies texts. They are also prevalent in biographies and sometimes found in science texts. Especially in the primary grades, some of the lessons for this text feature can be done first with narrative text and then transferred to expository text. This way, students can see how a timeline might be used with all types of text.

Graphs. A graph is a visual feature that succinctly presents information. A graph can condense data and/or display numeric information important to the text. It can also be used to compare amounts or show changes over time. There are three basic types of graphs: a circle or pie graph, a bar graph, and a line graph. A bar graph can sometimes utilize pictures in place of a bar and is then called a pictograph. The lessons in this section introduce students to graphs—specifically, circle/pie, bar, and pictographs—and cover their purpose, their parts, how to read them, how to use them to answer questions (to comprehend), and how to create them. Because bar graphs are so prevalent in elementary classrooms and reading texts, we have chosen to primarily focus on these types of graphs, although lessons could be adapted to the type of graph you are seeking to teach.

Charts/tables. Charts and tables are tools that can organize and condense large amounts of information or data into columns and rows with headings. They allow the reader to easily read and compare data, especially data related to the text. These tool can help illuminate important information from the text in a succinct way. Students will be required to use charts/tables throughout their academic career. The terms *chart* and *table* are often used interchangeably. For our lessons, we have chosen *table*, but either term could be used. We chose *table* because many classrooms have charts displayed in the classroom that do not fit the criteria we have described here and this may confuse students.

Purpose

To help students appreciate the importance of using a photograph or drawing in a text.

Prerequisite Skills

None

Materials

Various pictures and photographs

Directions

1. Ask, "Have you ever heard the expression, 'A picture is worth a thousand words?' Do you know what that means?" If students have no idea of the meaning, supply them with the meaning: "A picture can tell a story with little-to-no words."
2. Show students some pictures that tell a story without using words. These can be student generated or found from another appropriate source. See samples on the CD.
3. After showing a picture, ask students, "What story does this picture tell? What would you expect to read about based on this picture?" You should expect students to give you logical responses connecting a main idea to the picture you shared.
4. Repeat this process with another picture.
5. Wrap up the lesson: "We have looked at several different pictures and talked about what we would expect to read about if the author included a certain picture. Why would an author include a photograph or drawing?" Hopefully, someone will explain that pictures help the reader better visualize and/or understand something in the text. If not, explain this to students.

Modifications (for younger, less-able, or LEP students)

None

Assessment Options

Because this activity is directed by you, you will be using observation and questioning to assess understanding.

Technology

Use an interactive whiteboard or document camera to display images for this lesson.

Purpose

To help students understand that captions help the reader understand a picture.

Prerequisite Skills

Students should know what a picture is (photograph or drawing) and know what a caption or label is.

Materials

Pictures without a caption and the same pictures with a caption

Directions

1. Review, "Why do authors include pictures with their writing?"
2. Responses should explain that pictures help the reader see and better understand events, steps, or objects described in the text.
3. Yesterday we looked at pictures without captions. Show a picture with a caption and then one without a caption (see sample below).

Stuck in a shoe

4. Ask students, "How are these pictures the same and how are they different?" Hopefully someone will notice the caption. Read and talk about the caption, and then ask, "What does the caption tell us about the picture?" If students are unfamiliar with the word <u>caption</u> share a definition (a caption explains the feature—in this case, a picture—it is near). Ask students, "Did the way you think about the picture changed when you looked at the photo with the caption?" For example, in this photo, students may have thought the dog was playing with or chewing on the shoe. With the addition of the caption, the students should realize the dog was not supposed to be in the shoe and she/he got stuck inside it.
5. Try this same process with another picture.
6. Wrap-up lesson, and ask the student, "How does a caption add to a picture? Why would an author include a caption?"

Modifications (for younger, less-able, or LEP students)

Have students come up and point at the caption.

Assessment Options

Because this activity is directed by you, you will be using observation and questioning to assess understanding.

Technology

Use an interactive whiteboard or document camera to display images for this lesson.

Purpose

To review the role of pictures as a text feature, and to have students decide what picture would most closely relate to the main idea of a text.

Prerequisite Skills

Students should know what a picture is, and why authors include pictures in a text.

Materials

Thinksheet 3.1: Which Picture?, two drawings or photographs for step 2. These could be done ahead of time or you could do rough sketches in front of the students.

Directions

1. Review the purpose of pictures in stories.
2. Tell students a brief description of something you are going to write about (make it up or use the script below): "I am writing a story about going on vacation with my family to Clearwater Beach, Florida. I am going to describe how beautiful the weather was and what we did on the beach. Which picture would be most appropriate? Why?" One drawing could have palm trees, the sand and water, sunshine, and people in bathing suits wearing sunglasses. The other drawing could have palm trees, sand and water, lightning, rain and people in shorts and t-shirts carrying an umbrella. Discuss why the first picture would me more appropriate.
3. Now tell students that you want to write a story about going to Disney World with your family or you could identify a place you think the majority of your students have visited. Ask students, "What might be a good picture to go with my story?" As students share their ideas discuss why or why not the picture would be appropriate.
4. Then explain to students that they will be completing *Thinksheet 3.1*, where they will read a description of a story and then match the picture which would best go with that story. They will also be asked to draw a picture that goes with a brief description of a story.

Modifications (for younger, less-able, or LEP students)

Thinksheet 3.1 could be guided, or students could be paired with a stronger student who could assist with the reading.

Assessment Options

Because this activity is directed by you, you will be using observation and questioning to assess understanding.

Technology

Use an interactive whiteboard or document camera to display images and *Thinksheet 3.1* for this lesson.

Purpose

To help students recognize that inset photos are small, close-up pictures of a photo taken from far away. They help you see the details of a picture in the text.

Prerequisite Skills

Students should understand that photographs help the reader visualize something in the text.

Materials

Inset photo from Table 1.2

Directions

1. Use the inset photo in Table 1.2 on page 6 or find your own example. Cover the inset and show just the large picture. Ask, "What does the large photograph show?" They will (or should) say a fish. Ask, "What type of book might have a picture of a fish in it?" Guide a brainstorm of possible book topics. Student might say things like, "All About Oceans," "Fishing," or "I Love Lakes."

2. Next, reveal the inset and ask, "What does this show?" Ask students, "Why is this little picture of a fish tail overlapping the picture of the fish?" If they don't figure out that the tail is part of the fish, tell them that the tail is on the fish.

3. Explain (and point to the inset), "This small picture is a special type of text feature called an inset. It is connected with a larger picture that shows something in the text from far away. In this case, the larger picture shows an entire fish and the inset picture shows in an up-close view of the fish's tail."

4. Now ask students, "Think about what this text might be about considering it includes the fish tail inset." Possible answers include "What Are the Parts of a Fish?" or "Tropical Fish."

5. Ask students, "What kinds of things would you like to see close up?" Optional—you can chart these.

6. Review that an inset is a small close-up picture of something in a bigger picture.

Modifications (for younger, less-able, or LEP students)

- Supply possible titles and have students choose the ones they like for steps 1 and 4. Examples could be: "A Pretty Day," "Swimming in the Pool," "I Like Eggs," "Oceans," "A Dog Is a Man's Best Friend," and "Who Lives in an Ocean?"
- You could also put a word bank up on the board to assist with discussion. Possible words might include: ocean, lake, fish, tropical, habitat, etc.

Assessment Options

Because this is an initial inset lesson, it would be most appropriate to observe and assess the students who need a one-on-one or small-group follow up.

Technology

Use a document camera or projection screen to show the inset.

Purpose

To help students understand that insets show a close-up view of a larger picture.

Prerequisite Skills

Students must have been introduced to insets.

Materials

Sample of inset; *Thinksheet 3.2: Set in What?*

Directions

1. Show a sample of an inset with its larger photo and ask a student to point to the inset. Ask, "What is an inset, and why do books include them?" Students should say that insets show a close-up of a larger picture. They help us see what something looks like close up.

2. Show the large picture of a jungle. Ask students, "What might be an appropriate inset for this photo?" Possible answers might be a parrot, a tree, a frog, a large butterfly, etc. Ask, "Would a close-up picture of a bicycle be appropriate?" Lead a discussion about why this would not work well in the picture of the jungle.

3. Tell students, "Today you will be matching insets with larger pictures they go with." Hand out *Thinksheet 3.2.* Have students work in pairs. Instruct them to discuss what is in each picture and each inset, and then talk about which ones belong together. Have them draw a line matching the inset with its corresponding picture.

4. Have students cut the images out and glue them on paper as photos with insets. Have students write a brief caption under each inset to explain what is being shown. You will need to show them some real examples of insets so they see how they go together. A common format looks something like this:

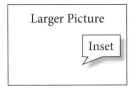

Captions should explain what is being shown, such as
"Close-up of a tire" or "A man's eye."

5. When students are done, discuss the choices they made and why they made them. Correct any misconceptions, and, once more, have students tell you what an inset is.

Modifications (for younger, less-able, or LEP students)

As a whole group, discuss what each large picture and inset on the page shows. Have students write a word under each picture to help them remember what it is. Make sure students are familiar with what the pictures depict and encourage them to ask if they are not.

Assessment Options

Collect these before the final discussion to see who understands insets and who does not.

Technology

Use a document camera or projection screen to show the inset.

Purpose

To help students find and read insets in texts.

Prerequisite Skills

Students must understand what an inset is and what it looks like. Students must be able to find the chapter title or section heading in a textbook.

Materials

Science textbook or trade books that include insets; *Thinksheet 3.3: Inset Hunt*

Directions

1. Review the definition and uses of an inset. Remind students that an inset is a small, close-up picture of a photo taken from far away and that it is attached to a larger photo in some way. Insets are used to show things close up.
2. Tell students that you can find many insets in science texts because the authors want us to see some things from both close up and far away.
3. You can choose to limit the inset hunt to a section or the entire textbook. Hand out the thinksheet and go over the directions, doing the first inset with students to model.
4. Have students work alone or with partners to find and analyze insets.
5. When students have each found four insets, pull the group together and discuss what they found. Ask, "Were there any common types of things that were shown in insets? What did you learn from looking at that inset? Why do you think they used insets in this section? How does that inset relate to the main idea of this section?"

Modifications (for younger, less-able, or LEP students)

- Limit the size of the section of text they will peruse and/or assign a specific page you know has an inset. You can also strategically pair students in mixed ability pairs. Scribe for students.
- Use this structure in small-group or one-on-one settings.

Assessment Options

Look at the thinksheet to determine if students can correctly identify insets.

Technology

On an interactive whiteboard, use an e-book version of the textbook and do as a whole class. Put the *Thinksheet 3.3* on the interactive whiteboard.

Purpose

To have students construct simple inset photographs.

Prerequisite Skills

Students must understand what insets are used for, and how they are constructed.

Materials

Digital camera or printouts of photos

Directions

1. Review what an inset is and why they are used.
2. Ask students to list some things they would like to see close up.
3. Tell students that today they will be making their own insets using a digital camera or printed pictures. (You will need to supply some broad-view and related close-ups for students to do this.)
4. Tell them that, for example, if you wanted someone to know what the whole school looks like as well as your classroom, you might take a photo of your school for the background picture and a photo of your classroom for the inset. Either print out these two images and physically show students how to put them together, or show the images on a projection screen and move them together using photo-editing software or even Microsoft Word. Optional—have students provide a caption for these.

5. Have students brainstorm far-away and close-up photographs they could take related to the classroom or school. Monitor students to ensure they are being realistic. Some examples might be the whole cafeteria and your seat in the cafeteria, or the entire playground and the sand or mulch in the playground. Have pairs of students decide what exactly they will photograph, or what pictures they will use from the collection provided.
6. If students are photographing things outside the classroom, take a mini-fieldtrip and allow each pair to take their photos as you go. If students are using provided photos, have them team up and cut and paste the photos into inset photos. Then, agree upon and write out captions to go with the photos and insets.
7. If students take pictures, this may need to be continued the next day so you can easily download photos. This second part could also be done as a center once photos are downloaded, depending on your students' technology knowledge. Have students manipulate photos using a drawing program, or print the pictures out for them and allow them to physically cut and paste the photos into insets. Make sure they write relevant captions for their insets. The end result can become a classroom book titled, *Our World, Close up and Far Away*, or something of the students' choosing.

Modifications (for younger, less-able, or LEP students)

- Make sure students understand what insets are before having them make one.
- Think about creating several insets as a whole class instead of having students work in pairs.

Assessment Options

Because we recommend this be done in partners, it is not the best assignment to grade. If you are using this for assessment purposes, you should pay attention to whether or not students put together related far away pictures and related close-up insets. Captions can also reveal how much students know about the purpose of insets.

Technology

Students can do image searches to find images they would like to use for an inset.

1. Teach them to save the picture, then open it again using an image editing program.
2. Have them use the cropping tool to select a section of the image they would like to see close up, crop it, then save the new cropped image as a separate file. They can resize this image or even crop it again to get up close.
3. Instruct students to copy the original picture and paste it to a Word document.
4. Have them insert a small text box next to or on the corner of the image in the Word document and insert the cropped image into the text box. Now they can move the inset anywhere on the larger image they would like.
5. Have students write a caption for the inset (see student example below).

A student created this inset with photos from a field trip.

This is the Castillo de San Marcos fort (above). It is the oldest Spanish building in Florida, it is 339 years old! This is a close up of a cannon that they shot cannonballs with (above right).

Purpose

To introduce students to the purpose of cross-sections.

Prerequisite Skills

None

Materials

An apple, an orange, paper, and crayons or pencils for the students

Directions

1. Ask students what a cross-section is. Explain that a cross-section helps us see the inside and all the layers or parts of an object.
2. Ask students what the inside of an apple looks like. They may say it is white or it has seeds.
3. Show students an intact apple. Using your paring knife, peel away a 1-inch diameter circle of peel so that students can see the flesh, but not the seeds, of the fruit.
4. Ask students if they can now see everything inside the apple. Someone may point out that there are seeds in the middle. If not, they will know soon!
5. Carefully cut the apple in half (either way will do) and show students the inside of the apple. Discuss what the inside of the apple looks like. Draw an example on the board. Tell students that features such as cross-sections usually have titles explaining what they show, and that a good title of this might be "Inside an Apple" or "Cross-section of an Apple." Write the title above your drawing on the board.
6. Show students an orange. Ask students what the inside of an orange looks like.
7. Ask students to draw a picture of what they predict the inside will look like when you cut the orange in half. Discuss their drawings.
8. Cut the orange in half in the middle (rather than naval to naval) so that you can see the sections of the orange. Show students the inside and ask if anyone would like to modify their predictive drawings. Allow them to do so.
9. Ask students what would be an appropriate title for the orange. They should come up with something like, "Cross-section of an Orange" or "Inside of an Orange." Ask students what other things they would like to see the inside of. Make a class list of their answers.
10. Review what a cross-section is.

Modifications (for younger, less-able, or LEP students)

Provide precut orange circles for students to use when creating their predictions of what will be inside an orange.

Assessment Options

Because this is the first lesson, it is most appropriate to observe and see who may need more lessons like this to understand the concept.

Technology

Use a document camera to display the cut fruit.

Using a digital camera, have students take photos of the cut fruit. Upload photos to a computer and have students either use a drawing program to add a title and label the parts of the fruit (such as skin, flesh, seeds), or print pictures for students and have them hand write a title and labels.

Cross section of a orngou

Purpose

To introduce students to the purpose of cross-sections, and to help students identify cross-sections.

Prerequisite Skills

Students should have a basic knowledge of cross-sections. They should know that cross-sections show the inside of an object and that they show something cut all the way through.

Materials

Fun-sized, layered candy bars (such as Milky Way or Snickers); plastic knives or a clay-sculpting knife

Directions

1. Review what you learned about cross-sections in the first lesson.
2. Tell students that today they are going to make cross-sections of mini candy bars. Have them read the candy bar labels to predict what the inside will look like when they cut it in a cross-section. Have them draw their predictions.
3. Show and tell students how to saw back and forth to slice through the bar instead of pushing down to cut it in half. Have students carefully cut cross-sections of their candy bars, then draw and label the actual inside.
4. Discuss the purpose of a cross-section title and have students write a title at the top.
5. Have students share their drawings and titles.

Modifications (for younger, less-able, or LEP students)

- Read and discuss the candy bar description from the label.
- Cut the candy bar for students who require help.

Assessment Options

Observe to see that the students' cross-section titles are appropriate.

Technology

Use a document camera to display a cut candy bar

Using a digital camera, have students take photos of the cut candy bar. Upload photos to a computer and have students either use a drawing program to add a title and label the layers (such as chocolate, caramel, and nougat), or print pictures for students and have them hand write a title and labels for the photograph.

Purpose

To have students find examples of cross-sections in text.

Prerequisite Skills

Students should be able to locate the title of a chapter or book, and they should have basic knowledge of cross-sections (i.e.: they should be able to show the inside of something or show something cut all the way through).

Materials

Non-fiction books with examples of cross-sections (both trade books and content-area texts work well—earth and life science topics usually include a bevy of cross-sections); *Thinksheet 3.4: Cross-section Hunt* made into large chart for the class

Directions

1. Review what students have learned about cross-sections.
2. Review how to find the title of a text or of a chapter in a longer text by having students point to the book title on a trade book and point to the chapter title in a textbook or non-fiction chapter book. Ask students why the titles are important and what they tell us.
3. Tell students that you have selected a set of texts that have cross-sections in them. They are to work with a partner to find a cross-section. They should write down the title of the cross-section and the page number they found the cross-section on in the left column of their recording sheets. In the right column, they should write down the title of the book and, if applicable, the chapter where they found the cross-section.
4. After each group has found a cross-section, have them share by showing their feature to the class. Record their data on the class chart.
5. Go through the class chart and lead a discussion about why each cross-section was included in that particular text.

Modifications (for younger, less-able, or LEP students)

- Carefully pair students so at least one of the students can read the titles and scribe in each group.
- Use a small group format for students who need extra support.

Assessment Options

Thinksheet 3.4 can be used individually (rather than in groups) for a grade, although it will only indicate that students can identify the feature and the title/chapter title.

Technology

Display examples and the thinksheet on the interactive whiteboard or document camera.

Purpose

To have students look at a photograph and a diagram of the same item and identify how they are similar and different, as well as when an author might use one over another; to introduce students to text features and labeled diagrams.

Prerequisite Skills

Students should know what a photograph and or picture is, as well as what a caption (or label) is.

Materials

Photograph and labeled diagram of the same item

Directions

1. Compare and contrast a labeled diagram of an item to a photograph of the same object. Have the items side by side. See this simple example with a flower:

Flower (Photograph)   Parts of a Flower (Labeled Drawing)

petal

stem

Have students brainstorm what the two pictures have in common and how they are different.

2. Ask, "If you were the author, when would you choose to use a photograph of the rose over a labeled diagram of a rose? Is one better than the other?" Students should point out that the labeled diagram teaches you what the flower is made of while the picture is really just an image. We want students to realize that an author would use one over another depending on his or her purpose (main idea), and we want them to know that one is not better than the other.

3. Share other comparison examples of labeled diagrams and photographs or drawings. Continue to prompt discussion using the questions in step 2.

4. Optional: Add a comparison of a labeled cross-section to the labeled photograph. Repeat the steps of this lesson by altering the prompt to be, "If you were the author, when would you choose to use a labeled diagram of _____ (you could do flower again) over a cross-section that is also a labeled diagram? Which is better?" Students should realize that with a labeled cross-section they can see the insides of the object in addition to knowing the names of the parts.

Modifications (for younger, less-able, or LEP students)

This lesson includes visuals and therefore is supportive to LEP learners.

Assessment Options

Because this activity is directed by you, you will be using observations and questioning to assess understanding. In addition, you could show a photograph and ask the students, "Is this a diagram?" Then, you can discuss why it is not a photograph if needed.

Technology

The entire lesson could be on an interactive whiteboard. The assessment piece could be done by having students text or use clickers to respond.

Purpose

To help students define, as well as know, the purpose and parts of a diagram.

Prerequisite Skills

Students must know what a diagram is and be familiar with some text features, such as pictures, captions, and labels.

Materials

A diagram or several different types of diagrams that you can show as examples (science textbooks have numerous diagrams) and that include all diagram parts (see example in Table 1.2 on CD)

Directions

1. Have students look at various diagrams. Have them notice parts of diagrams. This could be done in small groups or as a class. If students are in small groups, have them brainstorm a list of parts of diagrams and have them come together as a whole group.

2. Show the following diagram or another diagram, and ask students to brainstorm what the parts of the diagram may be. Write these parts onto sticky notes, index cards, or paper strips. It would be effective if you could also write on the diagram itself. Possible parts include: a title, labels, arrows, photographs, drawings, numbers, captions, and steps. Talk about each part as you label it on the diagram.

3. If you are not writing directly on the diagram, place each mini note (sticky note, index card, or paper strip) directly on the diagram. Discuss: "What is the purpose of each part? Do some parts have more than one purpose (arrows, for example)?"

4. Help students develop a definition for each part. This could become a resource in their reading folder or a class poster. If you have older students, the activity could be done by placing students in smaller groups. The goal would be to develop a common definition for the parts of a diagram.

5. Using a new diagram, ask students to identify different diagram parts.

Modifications (for younger, less-able, or LEP students)

Strategically partner students.

Assessment Options

Because this activity is directed by you, you will be using observation and questioning to assess understanding. If students work in small groups, you can observe by listening in and probing children for understanding. You could provide students with a diagram and have them label the parts correctly.

Technology

The entire lesson could be done on the interactive whiteboard.

Purpose

To review the parts of a diagram, and to get students to begin to read diagrams to answer questions. This lesson is most appropriate for grades two and up.

Prerequisite Skills

Students must know what a diagram is and have some knowledge of parts of a diagram.

Materials

Sample diagrams or a diagram of a life cycle of the Monarch from previous lessons/Table 1.2; poster with parts of a diagram from the previous lesson; "How to Read a Diagram" poster (on the CD; see directions in step 1—these can be modified with fewer words for students, and you may be able to use parts of a sample diagram as picture clues for students)

Directions

1. Use a think-aloud as you read a diagram.
    How to Read a Diagram (a poster of this can be created ahead of time—use "Graphic Features Activity 13_How to Read a Diagram Poster" on the CD for easy duplication)
    1. Read the title of the diagram. What does the title tell you about this diagram? What is this diagram trying to teach you?
    2. Read any text from the diagram. Look at the labels and captions. These are important words to notice. They tell you about the important parts of the diagram or explain parts of the diagram. The labels point to a specific part of the diagram with an arrow or line. The captions can be located under the diagram or under a part of the diagram. Think about how these words help you understand the diagram better.
    3. Look at the arrows and numbers that connect the pictures or drawings. These show what direction or order to read the diagram in.
    4. Read the text on the page before the diagram and the page after the diagram.
    5. Notice how the information is organized on the page. Think about how the diagram fits with what you are reading about in the main body of the text.
    6. If something in the diagram does not make sense, re-read it to clarify.
2. Review the steps of reading a diagram (see step 1 above). If you have not already, create a class poster with the steps of reading a diagram.

Modifications (for younger, less-able, or LEP students)

- Use picture clues with labels for the parts of a diagram.
- Also, strategically partner students for the assessment follow-up.

Assessment Options

Give students a diagram or have them locate one in a content textbook. Your best bet is to use a science text. Have students follow the steps with a partner, and have them read the diagram given by taking turns reading and then practicing the steps.

Technology

The teacher-directed portion of this lesson can be done on an interactive whiteboard. The poster can be displayed on the interactive whiteboard or using a document camera.

Purpose

To have students read a diagram and use the diagram to answer questions. The teacher-directed portion of this lesson would be appropriate for first graders but the assessment options are designed for grades 2 and up.

Prerequisite Skills

Students must know what a diagram is and be aware of the parts of a diagram. It would be helpful if they already had a lesson on how to read a diagram.

Materials

A projected or displayed (ideally enlarged) diagram, such as the one showing the life cycle of the Monarch butterfly from the previous lessons

Directions

1. Show students a diagram. If you are unable to locate one, use the Monarch butterfly life cycle diagram in Table 1.2.
2. Review the parts of a diagram. Guide students on how to read a diagram using the following prompts:
   a. What does the title tell us about this diagram? What do we expect to learn from the title?
      b. How should I read this diagram? Where does the diagram start? Where does the diagram end?
   c. How do the arrows help us read or understand the diagram?
   d. What do the captions and labels tell us?
3. Guide students to answer the questions using the diagram. If you are using the life cycle of the Monarch butterfly, you can use the following questions and answers:
      a. How does a Monarch butterfly begin? What is the first stage? <u>As an egg</u>
      b. What color is the pupa in the early stage? <u>Green</u>
      c. What happens to the pupa from the early stage to the later stage? <u>It becomes translucent and the butterfly begins to form its shape</u>
      d. Before it becomes a pupa, what is it? <u>A caterpillar</u>
4. Optional—have students create a new question that can be answered by reading the diagram.

Modifications (for younger, less-able, or LEP students)

- This is a teacher-directed activity, so the teacher can provide more scaffolding by prompting or redirect with feedback.
- Because the activity can be repeated with new diagrams, the teacher can strategically pair higher functioning students with those who need more support.

Assessment Options

Using the same format, this lesson can be repeated multiple times with different diagrams. Have students formally record responses or confer with students to determine mastery.

Technology

Already part of the lesson, but this could easily be done as a computer center activity.

Purpose

To familiarize students with and discuss the purpose of Venn diagrams.

Prerequisite Skills

Students should complete a Venn diagram of something familiar to them prior to doing this hands-on activity.

Materials

Two hula hoops; two jump ropes to make a Venn diagram or a pre-made Venn diagram poster; index cards or paper strips; optional—use picture cards to represent words for younger and LEP students

Directions

1. Show students a completed Venn diagram or create one based on something that is familiar to the students. This could be a comparison of two books they have read, such as a fairy tale and an adaptation of the same fairy tale, two books from the same author, or a comparison of teachers to students.
2. Ask students, "What do you notice about the Venn diagram?" Students should notice that there are two circles. Each circle represents ideas related to one topic. Point out that the circles overlap in the center and the ideas listed in the middle are what the two topics have in common.
3. Explain to students that they will be doing a Venn diagram. Place a Venn diagram on the board (or interactive whiteboard). You could also use two overlapping jump ropes or two hula hoops and place these on the floor. Determine your categories (the things you will be comparing and contrasting). Label each circle with an index card or paper strip. Have the labels represent the subjects of your Venn diagram. Label the area where the circles overlap with the word "both." For kindergarten students, you could use picture cards that are labeled. For example you could use cards of animals. One group could be pets, one could be animals you would find in a zoo, and the alike would be animals that could also be pets and in a zoo.
4. Next, have students brainstorm ideas for each category, or prepare examples for each category ahead of time. Tell students to place index or picture cards in the appropriate place in the Venn diagram and have them explain why they are putting the cards in chosen areas of the diagram
5. Tell students, "Today we made a Venn diagram. A Venn diagram shows the relationship between two or more items. It is a type of diagram. Diagrams provide us with details about something we are learning. Sometimes this includes steps that show us a process or how something is made. We will be learning about different types of diagrams and how to read these because they are important to understanding or clarifying something in the text."

Modifications (for younger, less-able, or LEP students)

Use pictures instead of words.

Assessment Options

Because this activity is directed by you, use observation and questioning to assess understanding.

Technology

An interactive whiteboard could be used to display Venn diagrams and complete the lesson.

Purpose

To have students create a diagram. This is not an appropriate exercise for students in kindergarten unless the lesson was completely teacher directed. For students in first grade or higher, have them use a thinksheet to plan and create their diagram and then the rubric to evaluate their diagram. As always, you will want to model how to create a diagram before they are asked to do this on their own.

Prerequisite Skills

This is a culminating activity for diagrams, so students must know what a diagram is and the parts of the diagram you are asking them to include.

Materials

Toothbrushes and toothpaste to demonstrate steps for brushing; materials related to your guided-practice topic that allow students to complete the task they are explaining (for example, if you choose, "Steps to Making a Peanut Butter Sandwich" as your topic, you would want a loaf of bread, peanut butter, plastic knives, paper plates, and napkins); *Thinksheet 3.5: Explain It! Creating a Diagram*; *Thinksheet 3.6: Diagram Rubric*; poster board or construction paper, along with other art supplies

Directions

Part I

1. Bring students in a group. Review the concept of a diagram. If needed, remind students that a diagram can explain steps in a process or how something is made. Ask students to think about when they brush their teeth. "What is the first thing you do when you brush your teeth?" Have students share ideas with you.

2. Explain that today you will be going to share with your students what you do when you brush your teeth. "The first thing I do is take my toothbrush out of the cup where it is displayed. Next, I pick up my toothpaste tube and screw off the cap of the toothpaste. Then, I squeeze the toothpaste tube and put a pea-sized amount of toothpaste onto the bristles (or head) of the toothbrush. I put my toothbrush under my bathroom faucet and turn the handle on and off to dampen the bristles (with the toothpaste) with some water. Next, I open my mouth and put the toothbrush in my mouth. I move the bristles up and down along all of my teeth, starting with my front teeth and then moving to the back of my teeth. When I have brushed all of my teeth, I spit what is in my mouth into the bathroom sink. Then I turn the bathroom faucet on and place the toothbrush into the running water to clean off the bristles. Lastly, I put my toothbrush back in my cup." These steps could be written down beforehand, or you could write them down as you are telling them to students. Leave numbers, a title, and any pictures off of the steps.

3. Review your written steps. Ask students, "What is missing from my steps?" Hopefully someone will identify that numbers, a title, and pictures are missing.

4. Say, "My steps need a title. What would be a good title for my steps?" Have students share ideas. Obviously something like "Steps to Brushing Teeth" would be best. Depending on students' responses you could discuss why one title might be better than another.

5. After giving the steps a title ask, "If I were going to give my steps to someone who has never brushed their teeth before how would they know where to start?" and then pause. "What do I need to do to my steps to help the reader know where to begin reading and where to end?" Hopefully someone will say number your steps. If not, tell them. Put numbers on each step.

6. Say, "Most of the diagrams we have been studying have pictures that go with what the diagram is explaining. Think about what pictures would be good for my diagram. Share with a partner what pictures you would expect to see on my 'Steps to Brushing Teeth.'" Pause and then say, "Let's look at step 1 (The first thing I do is take my toothbrush out of the cup where it is displayed). What would be a good picture for this step?" Continue through each step generating possible pictures for each step. Make sure that any illogical responses are not accepted.

7. Say, "Sometimes a picture in a diagram has a label or labels. That way, the reader can know the name of a part or parts. What label or labels might be helpful on my diagram? For example assuming that one of the pictures suggested was a toothbrush, show students a toothbrush and ask students, "Do you think everyone knows that the brushes of the toothbrush are called the head? We could label our picture of a toothbrush with the word head." You can continue and add any other labels you think might be helpful using the same questioning technique.

8. Wrap up the lesson by saying, "Today you helped me create a diagram 'Steps to Brushing Teeth'. Tomorrow you are going to work in teams to create your own diagram." Tell them what the topic will be (for example, "Making a Peanut Butter Sandwich").

Part II

1. Bring students together. Say, "Yesterday you helped me create a diagram called 'Steps to Brushing Teeth.' Today you are going to work in teams to create a diagram called 'Steps to Making a Peanut Butter Sandwich.' What are some parts of a diagram that you will need to include?" Have student share ideas, or provide them with the following suggestions: a title, numbered steps (explaining something), pictures to go with each step, and labels. Put these on a whiteboard or chart paper.

2. Say, "I am going to have you work in teams to create a diagram with these parts. You will also have a piece of bread, some peanut butter, and a plastic knife to help you make a peanut butter sandwich with your steps. The *Thinksheet 3.5: Explain It! Creating a Diagram* will help you organize your ideas.

3. Pair or group students. You will monitor students by observing and providing them with feedback. Most students will need some coaching, so you may want to have some volunteers or students from an older grade to come in and assist students in pairs or small groups.

4. After students have their discussion, bring the pairs or small groups back together. Have one group share its *Thinksheet 3.5: Explain It! Creating a Diagram*. Optional: Use the thinksheet students made for the "Making a Peanut Butter Sandwich" activity. If a step is missing or needs clarifying, revise it. Explain, "Next you need to revisit your thinksheet because you are going to create a poster of your 'Steps to Making a Peanut Butter Sandwich.'" Optional: Introduce *Thinksheet 3.6: Diagram Rubric* at this point. See assessment options.

5. Have students make their posters. It may be wise to have them write everything in pencil first, or have them type their suggestions in a document on the computer. After editing, they can color and decorate the poster.

Modifications (for younger, less-able, or LEP students)

The hands-on aspects of this lesson will be helpful for all learners. Strategically pair students or place them in small groups.

Assessment Options

During the whole class lesson and guided practice, observation and feedback will be critical. Use the rubric to have students create their own diagram. The rubric can be adapted depending on you expectations. For example, you may not require students to use labels so you could remove that row from the rubric.

Purpose

To define a map, its parts, and its purpose.

Prerequisite Skills

Students must have been exposed to a map or have access to maps. Knowing right from left and top from bottom would be helpful.

Materials

Maps, an atlas, brochures with maps, or any driving directions with a map that you have from an Internet map site; a set of five to ten books with maps in them or a grade-level textbook for science or social studies (enough so that students can work in pairs with a book/text)

Directions

1. Bring students to a class meeting area. Ask if they have ever driven with their family to a new or unfamiliar place and how they knew where they were going. Someone may say they used a map. If no one says this, probe further by adding, "When you went to a new place or unfamiliar area, you might have had directions that were written down, or a GPS (Global Positioning System) that told you which way to turn, how far you would have to drive, and how long the trip would take. Or you may have just used a map like this (hold up an example of a map, preferably one that is poster size when unfolded or projected from the Internet. A good source for maps is www.worldatlas.com/aatlas/world.htm)."

2. Show children different types of maps. These can be paper and/or electronic.

3. Say, "These are all maps," then ask "What is a map?" Answers might explain that a map shows where something is, shows towns, shows mountains, shows lakes and oceans, or is a picture that shows where something or someone is located. If students cannot answer this, use one of the maps you showed them and tell them a map is a picture showing the geographic location of something or someone. For older students, you can show them different types of maps (like a weather map, population map, or political map) and discuss how they are alike and different.

4. Ask students to share verbally or, if developmentally appropriate, write down why maps are important. Their responses may include that they help keep you from getting lost, help you get somewhere, and show you where things are located. If students have a hard time with this concept, you may want to go back to step 1 and talk about a time students went somewhere new or unfamiliar. If they cannot come up with an example, provide one from your life.

5. Tell students maps are also found in books. Ask them if they have ever seen a map in a book, and show an example. You could project the example with a document camera, scan it onto a computer, or show the map in a read-aloud format. Discuss using think-aloud why the author chose to put that map in that book/text.

6. Have students work in small groups with the set of books you pre-selected or their content-area textbook. Have them be detectives and locate a map with an elbow partner. Walk about the room. When students have located a map, have them raise their hand and check for understanding. Once they have found a map, you can have them talk about why they think the map is in their book/text.

7. When everyone has located a map, ask them why they think the author put that map in the book or textbook they are looking at. Some responses might include: a. to show you where something or someone in the text is located, b. to help you quickly know the location of something in the text, or c. to help you see the impact of something based on geographic location.

8. If students are unable to supply a reason or reasons why the author may have included a map, share another example (you can use the one you shared in step 5) and use think-aloud to lead them to the answers in step 7 (7.c. would be more appropriate for older students).

Modifications (for younger, less-able, or LEP students)

See modifications within the lesson directions.

Assessment Options

Have students respond orally to the following sentence frames (older students can fill in the blanks).

A map is a _____

_____.

Maps are important because _____

_____.

An extension activity could be to have students complete the following sentence frames doing a map hunt in one of the books you used in the main lesson.

My map is of _____

_____.

My map is important because _____

_____.

I think the author put this map in the text because _____

_____.

Technology

Steps 1–5 could be accomplished using an interactive whiteboard.

Purpose

To review what a map is, explain its purpose, and introduce parts of a map.

Prerequisite Skills

Students should already have an idea of what a map is and why they are important. This lesson would be most appropriate for first grade and up, but kindergarteners who understand these concepts may be ready for this lesson.

Materials

Maps (at least one map with a title, key/legend, compass rose, and scale); *Thinksheet 3.7: Parts of a Map: What Am I?*; optional—parts of a map (title, key/legend, compass rose, and scale) on sticky notes and a ruler (see steps 2–5)

Directions

1. Review what a map is and the purpose of a map (a map shows the location of something or someone). Show a map. Ask, "What is this?" Ask, "Why are maps important?" Using a map, go over its parts in a think-aloud format: title, latitude and longitude (optional), key or legend, scale, and pointer or compass rose). Read the title of the map: _____
    _____. If possible, write or type the word title next to or near the title of the map you are using. If you are using an interactive whiteboard, you can write directly on the map which part you are showing or you could have the parts pre-written sticky notes that you place on the part as you teach it.
    a. *Title*: Say, "The title should give you the main idea or purpose of the map." If the students are older, ask them what they think the purpose of the title is. What does the title tell us about this map?"
    b. *Key or Legend*: Point to the key or legend of the map. Say, "The key or legend is usually in a box in one of the corners of the map. It gives you the information you would need to understand what the colors and symbols on the map mean. You do not always have to read a word in the key or legend to know what it is because the author uses a symbol to stand for the word. A symbol can be anything like a drawing, line, or a dot. Sometimes it is just the use of a different color." If possible, write these terms so all students can see them on the map (or use sticky notes). Go over the key or legend for the map you are using in the lesson. Optional—enlarge the symbols for the map you are using on different sticky notes.
    c. *Scale:* Point to the scale of the map. Say, "The scale looks like a ruler (you may want to have a ruler and demonstrate). It shows what the distance is between places on the map. It shows how the mapmaker chose to show the distance on a map. A map cannot be five miles across so the mapmaker chose a shorter distance to represent the distance, like an inch for every five miles." If possible, write this term so all students can see them on the map (or place sentence strip). Go over the scale for the map you are using in the lesson and demonstrate how to use the scale to estimate distance. You should demonstrate the concept of scale by discussing how if you were to create a map of the classroom you would not be able to find a piece of paper big enough to be the actual size of the classroom so instead you might use an inch to equal 3 ft. You can even use tape to compare three feet to one inch.

d. *Pointer or Compass Rose*: Point to the pointer or compass rose of the map. Say, "The pointer or compass rose helps you know the direction of places on the map. The pointer or compass rose always faces north." If possible, write these terms so all students can see them on the map (or place on sentence strip). Go over the key or legend for the map you are using in the lesson. Optional—place an enlarged compass rose in your classroom so students can see the direction your classroom faces: www.enchantedlearning.com/geography/printouts/compassrose.shtml.

e. (This step is optional and should be done if developmentally appropriate.) *Latitude and Longitude*: *Say, "Most maps have lines that run across (horizontally) and lines that go up and down (vertically). These lines are called lines of latitude and longitude." If possible, write these terms so all students can see them on the map (or place a sentence strip). Say, "The latitude and longitude lines tell you where the map is located on earth." You can also identify where the location of the map you are using is relative to the Earth by using a globe or map of the world.

f. Review the parts of the map: tile, key or legend, scale, and pointer or compass rose.

Modifications (for younger, less-able, or LEP students)

You may want to skip step 2.e.

Assessment Options

Give students a map. Remove any obvious labels for the parts, such as the word scale or legend. Put blanks for students to write in the parts. You may provide a word bank to the students. See sample *Thinksheet 3.7: Parts of a Map: What Am I?*.

Technology

This entire lesson can be done on an interactive whiteboard and would allow for you to mark up the map as you teach the parts.

Purpose

To review the parts of a map and to get children to begin to read maps to answer questions.

Prerequisite Skills

Students must know what a map is and must have been introduced to the parts of a map.

Materials

A map (or completed Thinksheet 3.7: Parts of a Map: What Am I? from previous lesson)

Directions

1. Give students a map and have them label the parts of the map: title, key or legend, scale, and pointer or compass rose. You could use *Thinksheet 3.7: Parts of a Map: What Am I?* or another map.
2. Review the parts of a map, checking for understanding.
3. Explain that a map needs to be read just like the main body of text needs to be read. Using a common (shared) map, have students answer the following probes (note probes may have to be adjusted to the map you are using):
   a. What is the title of the map?
   b. After reading the title what do you think the purpose of this map is?
   c. What does the color _____ mean for this map?
   d. What does the symbol _____ mean for this map?
   e. What does the scale tell you about this map?
   f. Take a moment and look at the map. Read the map. What have you learned from reading this map?
4. Extension activities in this lesson might include reading a weather map or reading a rain forest map.

Modifications (for younger, less-able, or LEP students)

This is a more teacher-directed lesson. The extension activities listed in step 4 could be done in small groups or with strategic partners.

Assessment Options

Using a new map, ask the students the same or similar probes listed in 3. Have students visit this site, www.tv411.org/lessons/cfm/reading.cfm?str=reading&num=8&act=4&que=1, and check through the interactive activities, or lead students through the activities on a projected screen or interactive whiteboard. This could be a literacy center once taught.

Technology

The entire lesson could be accomplished on an interactive whiteboard.

Purpose

Have students create a map.

Prerequisite Skills

Students must know what a map is, and know the parts of the map you are asking them to include on their map.

Materials

Sample map (with parts of map labeled) made on the computer using Paint/another drawing program or on paper, and hung nearby as you model making a map using the classroom as an example; sample maps available as resources for students to refer to while they are creating their own map; *Thinksheet 3.8: Creating a Map; Thinksheet 3.9: Map Rubric*

Directions

Part I

*Note: In kindergarten you may want them to only draw the map and include a title for the map. Then in first grade and up, you may want students to use the rubric to create their map. As always, you will want to model how to create a map before they are asked to do this on their own.

1. Explain to students that you are going to create a classroom map together. Have sticky notes or index cards available. With students, brainstorm a list of items in your classroom: teacher's desk, student desks, chairs, computers, classroom library, and so on. Place each item on a separate sticky note or index card. Students can assist with this by writing the item on each sticky note or index card, or you can write. The sticky notes or index cards will represent the items you brainstormed.
   Note: It may be more developmentally appropriate to have students do the classroom map in a 3-D model using small snap cubes (like Unifix Cubes) to represent items.
2. Draw an outline of the shape of your classroom on a piece of chart paper or on the board (this can be done on an interactive whiteboard as well). Explain to your students that this will be the map of our classroom.
3. Remind students, "A map should have a title that explains the map's purpose." Brainstorm a list of titles for the classroom map. Choose a title together and place this at the top of the map.
4. Give each child a sticky note or index card based on the items you brainstormed together.
5. Ask students, "What part of the map tells us the direction of the map?" If they do not recall compass rose, remind them. Decide which way is north in your classroom and this is how you will orient the map. You can put the compass rose on then or wait to add this as a finishing touch.
6. Call each student up to place their sticky note or index card on the classroom map so that it matches where they are found in the classroom. You will more than likely have to help them with placement of items. You might even want to model the placement of the first item like the door entry way. Continue placing sticky notes or index cards of items that were brainstormed in step 1.
7. Say, "Now our map would look pretty silly if we just kept sticky notes on it. What do you think we should do next?" If the students do not offer some suggestions related to drawing where each item is on the paper/board, you will need to step in. Say, "We have learned that maps

usually have a key or legend where symbols represent things on the map. Maybe we should come up with some symbols to represent items in our classroom and use those symbols on our map where each sticky note or index card is placed. What could we use for symbols?" Some possible symbols could be a square for desks, an "X" for chairs, a book for the classroom library. Decide on symbols, and make a draft of your key/legend, which will be placed on the map.

8. Pick up one of the sticky notes/index cards and ask what symbol you will put there while pointing to the location of the sticky note/index card. After a correct response, draw the symbol. To make this more interactive, you could have students draw the symbol on the map. Continue until all of the sticky notes/index cards have been replaced by a symbol.

9. Complete the map by adding the compass rose and key/legend if not already added.

Part II

1. Explain that students will now create their own map. Students can create a map as a small group or individually. Your teacher judgment will play into this decision.

2. Brainstorm the places students could make a map of. Some ideas might include the school, their neighborhood, or their favorite room in their house.

3. Have students use *Thinksheet 3.8: Creating a Map* to help them with their planning. This sheet can be adapted based on what map concepts you want them to include.

4. *Thinksheet 3.9: Map Rubric* can be used to evaluate maps.

Modifications (for younger, less-able, or LEP students)

In Part II, students could be strategically paired as to support all learners.

Assessment Options

See *Thinksheet 3.9: Map Rubric*. The rubric can be adapted based on your expectations. You can eliminate rows (criteria) that you do not expect students to use on their map.

Technology

The entire teacher-directed lesson (part I) can be done on an interactive whiteboard. Students can create their map using a computer program like Kid Pix or Paint.

Purpose

To teach students the purpose and importance of timelines (appropriate in grades one and up).

Prerequisite Skills

Students should have a general concept of beginning, middle, and end and know what a picture is.

Materials

Summary of *The Three Little Pigs* story on chart paper or interactive whiteboard (see lesson below); *Thinksheet 3.10: Three Little Pigs Timeline*; other timeline examples (including Table 1.2 example in Chapter 1 and on CD for older readers)

Directions

1. Read *The Three Little Pigs* retold by James Marshall, or a similar version of *The Three Little Pigs*. Have students retell the story or have a summary of the story on a chart (or an interactive whiteboard).
2. What would happen if we started the retelling the story with the wolf falling into a pot of boiling water, and then blowing down the house made of straw? What is wrong? Does it make sense? Hopefully they will say it does not make sense because the story needs to be told in the order that it happened.
3. Show students some different timelines (see Table 1.2 in Chapter 1 and on the CD for an intermediate example).
4. You can have the story of *The Three Little Pigs* in a timeline format—see *Thinksheet 3.10: Three Little Pigs Timeline*. Say, "Each of these is a timeline." Ask students, "What is a timeline?" If students are unable to tell you, say, "A timeline tells when things happened in the order they happened." You can stop at this definition or add, "It might tell the order something is done in. A timeline can show events that happen in someone's life in the order they took place. Along with dates and brief, relevant information, timelines can also include pictures."
5. Say, "Timelines have parts. What parts do you notice on the timelines?" Some responses might include a title (explains the timeline, what it shows), a line or an arrow, this is where the events or things are plotted onto, in order from oldest to most recent, pictures and words (these explain the events or things on the timeline).
6. "Our timeline for *The Three Little Pigs* does not have pictures. What pictures might we add to our timeline? Have students brainstorm ideas. If you want, have them add illustrations.
7. Review what a timeline is, including the purpose and the parts to a timeline. You can label these parts with one of the timeline examples.

Modifications (for younger, less-able, or LEP students)

- Pictures can be added to the Three Little Pigs retelling chart to assist children with reading the retelling chart.
- Examples include a picture of pigs instead of the word pig and a picture of a house made of straw instead of the word straw.

Assessment Options

Because this activity is directed by you, you will use observation and questioning to assess understanding.

Technology

Use the interactive whiteboard to display Thinksheet 3.10.

Purpose

To teach students how to read a timeline. This activity can be modified for kindergarten students.

Prerequisite Skills

Students should know what a timeline is and its purpose.

Materials

Thinksheet 3.11: The History of Candy in America Timeline

Directions

1. Use *Thinksheet 3.11: The History of Candy in America Timeline* to review a timeline. You can do this as a whole group or each student can have his/her own copy to complete. If on an interactive whiteboard, have students draw a line from the image to where it belongs on the timeline.

2. Make sure students have the timeline in the correct order. Pose the following questions (this can be done using clickers):
    1. According to the timeline, what was the first candy in America? <u>Penny Candy</u>
    2. According to the timeline, when was candy corn invented in America? <u>1880</u>
    3. According to the timeline, what candy was invented in 1875? <u>Milk chocolate</u>
    4. What is your favorite candy and why? <u>It does not have to be on the timeline. Answers will vary.</u>

Modifications (for younger, less-able, or LEP students)

Use pictures only for timelines instead of pictures with words.

Assessment Options

Because this activity is directed by you, use observation and questioning to assess understanding. Follow-up could include repeating this activity with different timelines to determine whether students understand how to read and answer questions about timelines.

Technology

Use the interactive whiteboard for Thinksheet 3.11. As a follow-up activity, students could locate timelines on the Internet and develop their own questions for classmates to answer.

Purpose

To have students create a classroom timeline in order to better understand the concept of a timeline. This could be done in the first month of school and then added onto throughout the school year. This lesson is appropriate for grades one and up and can be completed as a whole class or in small groups.

Prerequisite Skills

Students need to know what a timeline is and the parts of a timeline.

Materials

Butcher block paper; markers; sticky notes or index cards

Directions

1. Explain to students that you are going to create a classroom timeline that you will be adding to throughout the school year. Review the important features of a timeline. Using butcher block paper or the whiteboard draw a horizontal line with an arrow.
2. Ask students what a good title would be for the timeline. Place the agreed upon title at the top of the timeline.
3. Divide the timeline into even segments for each month of the school year, although you may want to include summer months too as you may put students' birthdays on this timeline and you do not want any children to feel left out. Label these segments with each month beginning with the month you are in.
4. Plot student birthdays, holidays, and school vacations on the timeline. You may have to have students do some searching on the Internet to find out dates for school vacations and holidays. Have students suggest pictures to go with these events. Write these on sticky notes or index cards so that you can have students create the pictures as a follow-up activity.
5. Add school and community events. Have students suggest pictures to go with these events. Write these on sticky notes or index cards so that you can have students create the pictures as a follow-up activity. Some ideas include: For each new read-aloud, you can make a book cover to go on the timeline, or when a new unit of study is launched, you could mark this on the timeline with an appropriate picture.
   Note: Some ideas for pictures could include having students bring in a picture of themselves to be placed on their birthday or having students take pictures using a digital camera in your classroom. For school events, you could have students take appropriate pictures. For holidays, students could draw pictures or find them online.
6. Divvy up the sticky notes or index cards and have students create pictures to go with events on the timeline.

Modifications (for younger, less-able, or LEP students)

Provide peer tutors to help students determine appropriate placement.

Assessment Options

Use observation and questioning to assess understanding.

Technology

Students can use digital cameras, a scanner, or online resources to obtain pictures and research school events and holidays.

Purpose

To give students more practice with creating timelines using a read-aloud (a common text). (Note: This lesson is appropriate for grades one and up, although some modifications would be needed for first-grade students.)

Prerequisite Skills

Students must have been exposed to a timeline and its purpose.

Materials

Wilma Unlimited: How Wilma Rudolph Became the World's Fastest Woman by Kathleen Krull; *Thinksheet 3.12: Timeline Organizer* for each child, projected as a shared writing activity or on a poster; paper; colored pencils and/or crayons

Directions

1. Read a biography with your students. This lesson uses *Wilma Unlimited: How Wilma Rudolph Became the World's Fastest Woman* by Kathleen Krull, but you can use any biography.
2. After reading, have the class generate important events in the person's life (good and bad) using *Thinksheet 3.12: Timeline Organizer* (5 to 10 events). At this point, they do not need to be in order, so the first column of the thinksheet can be done later in the lesson if you choose. If you read *Wilma Unlimited*, your list of events might include (not in order): She got polio when she was a little girl, She could not go to school like other children because of her polio, She loved basketball and could run very fast, She was a runner in the 1960 Olympics, She had 19 brothers and sisters, She was determined to walk again, She was born very tiny in 1940 in Clarksville, Tennessee, She loved to go to church on Sundays.
3. Pair students up. Give each pair an event from *Wilma Rudolph* (see step 2) or from the biography you read. Have them create an illustration for each event. From grade one and up, students could create a caption to go on the illustration. This could be a label or a complete sentence about the event.
4. When all of the illustrations (and captions) are complete, arrange the pictures in order to make a timeline of Wilma's life (you may want to number the pictures on the back). Complete column one of the thinksheet. Suggest students write the number on the back of each illustration. The timeline can become a hallway or classroom bulletin board, or you can make it a "living timeline" by presenting it as a readers' theatre-type presentation in other classrooms." If you choose to have the students present their timeline, you will want them to write their caption or sentence on a sticky note that they place on the backside of their illustration, so they can read from it but show their illustration at the same time.
5. This activity can be repeated with other biographies as desired.

Modifications (for younger, less-able, or LEP students)

Strategically pair a less-able student with a more-able student (beginning with step 3).

Assessment Options

Use observation and questioning to assess understanding, as well as their completed illustration and any follow-up.

Technology

An interactive whiteboard can be used for the first part of this lesson (steps 1–2). The pictures for the second part of the lesson can be obtained online.

Thinksheet 3.12: Timeline Organizer   Name: _____

Use this table to record information for your timeline.

Number/order of events	Date/year	Event	Picture or symbol

Purpose

To give students more practice with creating timelines using their life experiences.

Prerequisite Skills

Students should know what a timeline is and its purpose. They should also have taken part in creating at least one class timeline.

Materials

Thinksheet 3.12: Timeline Organizer; pre-made timeline of your life—you can use the tool available at www.readwritethink.org/files/resources/interactives/timeline (provided by ReadWriteThink.org, a Thinkfinity website developed by the International Reading Association, the National Council of Teachers of English, and in partnership with the Verizon Foundation); a word-processing program or PowerPoint and several photographs from different times in your life (see step 1) to create your timeline; *Thinksheet 3.13: Timeline Rubric*

Directions

1. Show students a picture of when you were young, maybe a baby picture. Then show them a picture of when you were in elementary school. Show a picture of you from college. Then show them a current picture of you. Tell them a little bit about your life at the time of each photograph. OR show students your completed timeline and share each segment of your timeline. If desired, you can add a label or sentence to go with your picture.

2. Explain to your students that your timeline does not include everything from your life. You have only highlighted key events from your life. Explain that they will be creating a timeline of key events from their life.

3. Pass out *Thinksheet 3.12: Timeline Organizer* to students. Brainstorm with students what might be key events in their life, such as: when they were born, their first birthday, places they have moved to, when they went to pre-school, when they entered school, when a sibling was born, favorite vacations, special events (sports or hobbies), or pets. Have them turn their paper over so they can copy down ideas. The thinksheet will prompt them to write down the date of an event, to describe the event, and use pictures to match the event.

4. Completing the timeline thinksheet can be started at home, but they will probably want to verify information with someone at home. Encourage students to bring in mementos and photographs related to their events.

5. Provide time in class, or have students complete their timeline as an at-home activity based on their timeline thinksheet. Remember students can access online tools to construct their timeline. When the timelines are completed, mount them on the wall and have each child explain his or her timeline to the class.

Modifications (for younger, less-able, or LEP students)

Pair students strategically for steps 2–3. If needed, students can draw a picture of the event instead of using words.

Assessment Options

Use *Thinksheet 3.13: Timeline Rubric* to assess student timelines.

Technology

Use this template for students' final products: www.readwritethink.org/files/resources/interactives/timeline/ (provided by ReadWriteThink.org, a Thinkfinity website developed by the International Reading Association, the National Council of Teachers of English, and in partnership with the Verizon Foundation).

Purpose

To familiarize students with, and discuss the purpose of, a graph.

Prerequisite Skills

Students should be able to read some sight words and have some number sense. Additionally, they should know what a title is and be familiar with what a label is.

Materials

A textbook or trade book with various graphs or a worksheet with a variety of graphs on it; chart paper or whiteboard; sticky notes with the labels, "pie/circle," "bar," and "pictograph"

Directions

1. Show students a variety of graphs: a circle/pie, bar, and pictograph. Ask students what they think each graph is called, or what they have in common. If they are unable to identify them as graphs tell them and provide them with a definition. "A graph is a visual that shows numeric information, compares amounts, or shows changes over time. Graphs are often taught in math and when a graph is part of what we are reading, this means the author is using it to point out or demonstrate something important to the text."

2. Ask students what they notice about the graphs you have shown them, how are they alike and how are they different? They may differentiate the graphs by the shape, one is a circle or looks like a pie, one has bars or thick lines, another has pictures. They may notice the parts of each graph (such as a title, key, labels, pictures, and so on). Depending on their response(s)/background knowledge, you can decide what direction to take the lesson. We recommend you focus on distinguishing the types circle/pie, bar, and pictograph first, then hit on the parts (the focus of the next lesson, "The Anatomy of a Graph" will do this).

3. Label each type of graph (circle/pie, bar, and pictograph) then explain the differences depending on their brainstorming in step 2. Note: you can use premade labels or sticky notes to do this.

4. Review the types of graphs. If you can, project different graphs and have students identify the types. This would work well with clickers/polling, where students match the type (label) to the graph. If you do not have interactive whiteboard technology available, you can have sticky notes with the graph types listed (circle/pie, bar, and pictograph). Then ask for volunteers to match the correct sticky-note label to the correct graph.

Modifications (for younger, less-able, or LEP students)

A picture label could be placed with the graph types as a visual cue.

Assessment Options

Observe students and give immediate corrective feedback.

Technology

This lesson can be done effectively on an interactive whiteboard, per the lesson description.

Purpose

To review what a graph is, the purpose of a graph, the three types of graphs, and the parts of a graph: title, legend, axis labels.

Prerequisite Skills

Students must know what a graph is and be familiar with some text features such as titles, pictures, captions, and labels.

Materials

Sticky notes with the parts of a graph written on them; sample graphs from a text (you can reuse the graphs you used for the "What Is a Graph?" lesson); *Thinksheet 3.14: The Anatomy of a Graph: What Am I?*

Directions

1. Review with students what a graph is: "A graph is a visual that shows number information, compares amounts, or shows changes over time. Graphs are often taught in math and when a graph is part of what we are reading the author is using it to show us important information." See lesson "What is a graph?" for more guidance. Say, "Today we are going to learn about the parts of graphs." Written below are the parts of the graph that will be taught.
   a. Title: The graph title is located at the top of a graph. It tells what the graph is about.
   b. Two axes labels: Each graph has two axes, one across the bottom of the graph and one that is on the side of the graph. These are labeled. The labels tell us what information is on each axis.
   c. Legend or scale: The legend or scale is the amount on the side axis.
2. Hand to student volunteers the parts of a graph written on sticky notes. As you hand out the parts explain what they are and show an example using a graph that all the children can see. The graphs in the "What is a Graph?" lesson would work well here, too.
3. Display another graph so all students can see it. Ask the student volunteers to come up front with the graph part labels. Have each student show the class the label and then have the class identify where to place the sticky-note label of the graph part.
4. Review the parts of the graph and their purpose.

Modifications (for younger, less-able, or LEP students)

Re-teach this lesson in a small-group setting.

Assessment Options

Observe students while conducting the lesson to provide corrective feedback.

Technology

Graphs could be projected through an interactive whiteboard or similar tool.

Purpose

To have students read a graph to answer questions. The teacher-directed portion of this lesson would be appropriate for first graders, but the assessment options are designed for grades 2 and up.

Prerequisite Skills

Students must know what a graph is and the parts of a graph.

Materials

Various graphs; one bar graph enlarged for the whole class to view; *Thinksheet 3.15: Reading and Answering Questions about a Graph*

Directions

1. Review the purpose of a graph and the parts of a graph. Again, the lessons, "What is a Graph?" and "The Anatomy of a Graph" offer support for teaching these concepts.
2. Show students an example of different types of graphs. Those most prevalent in elementary school texts would be circle/pie, bar, and pictograph. Review the names of these graphs.
3. Choose one type of graph. This lesson suggests a bar graph. Show students a bar graph. Say, "Today I am going to think aloud and share the steps I follow when reading a graph."
4. "When I read a bar graph, the first thing I do is find and read the title of the graph. The title should give me an idea of what the subject of the graph is. The title of this graph is _____. Based on this title, I think the graph is about _____. Next, I look for and read the axes and think about how these relate to the title of the graph." Read these aloud, along with the title of the graph, and share your thinking with your students. If you have not already done so, read and share what the bars represent. If the graph has a legend/scale, think aloud about what this tells you in relation to what the bars represent.
5. If desired, pose questions about your graph. You may want to jump right to *Thinksheet 3.15: Reading and Answering Questions about a Graph*. This could be projected or students could have their own copies of this thinksheet. Facilitate discussion as students read and answer questions.
6. Review the importance of reading a graph. You may want to create a "How to Read a Graph" poster for your students to refer to. You can use the steps in this lesson as a starting point.

Modifications (for younger, less-able, or LEP students)

Have a printed copy of the graph for students to keep on their desks and refer to.

Assessment Options

Observation, *Thinksheet 3.15*, and the follow-up activities listed in the technology section of this lesson.

Technology

Complete Thinksheet 3.15 on the interactive whiteboard. You can find pre-made graphs online your students can read and answer questions about.

Purpose

To have students create a class favorites graph and then make their own. This would not be appropriate for students in kindergarten unless completely teacher directed. In first grade and up you may want students to use a thinksheet to plan and create their graph and the rubric to evaluate their graph. As always, you will want to model how to create a graph before they are asked to do this on their own.

Prerequisite Skills

Students must know what a graph is and know the parts of the graph you are asking them to include. Adapt the rubric according to the parts you want to include.

Materials

Thinksheet 3.16: Creating a Favorites Graph or *Thinksheet 3.17: What's Your Favorite*_____*?*; *Thinksheet 3.18: Graph Rubric*

Directions

1. Create a class "Favorite" graph. Choose a topic, such as favorite colors. Say, "Today we are going to make a class graph of what our favorite colors are." Use *Thinksheet 3.16: Creating a Favorites Graph* or *Thinksheet 3.17: What's Your Favorite* _____*?* to record students' favorite colors. One lesson option could be to ask students what different forms of transportation they use to come to school. Draw a bar graph on a large sheet of paper based on the categories they identify. Use a picture in each bar column to represent each transportation category. Then ask each child to write his name on a small sheet of paper and glue it onto the appropriate column. Children can graph their favorite snacks, books, songs, or animals. Alternatively, ask children to find out from family members about their favorite colors, books, or animals for each family member. Have them gather this information and bring this to school to create a graph.

2. Tally student's favorite colors (or whatever you choose to chart). Think aloud as you do this.

3. "Now we are going to take our data and create a graph." You can use *Thinksheet 3.16* or you can just draw one on the whiteboard. Ask, "First we need a title. What is our graph about? What would be a good title for our graph?" Write or type the title. Next, say, "A bar graph has two axes." Draw these. Say, "If the subject of our graph is favorite colors what needs to go at the bottom of our graph?" Point to the horizontal axis. Write the colors going across. Ask, "What should go on the vertical axis?" You can decide how you want to model the amounts that will go on the vertical axis. This will be based on your data amounts and the age of your students.

4. Now that your graph is completed you can review the steps to creating a graph, then explain, "Now you will be creating a graph of favorites on a different subject."

5. A follow-up to this lesson is to model how to create questions that can be answered from reading the graph. For example, from the favorite color graph you could ask, which color is liked the most and which color is liked the least?

Modifications (for younger, less-able, or LEP students)

- Pictures to go with the subject of the graph could be used.
- For step 4, students could be strategically paired or grouped.
- You could also use pre-cut pictures and have students make a pictograph.

Assessment Options

Use *Thinksheet 3.18: Graph Rubric* to evaluate students' graphing skills, step 4.

Technology

Use the interactive whiteboard or student computers to complete and then print Thinksheets 3.16 and 3.17. You could also model using technology to create a graph.

Purpose

To familiarize students with, and discuss the purpose of, a chart/table.

Prerequisite Skills

Students would benefit from previous knowledge of graphs. Many of the skills associated with graphs would transfer to this lesson.

Materials

A textbook or trade book with a table (examples of charts/tables and graphs) or the sample table presented in the lesson; chart paper or whiteboard; sticky notes to label the table used in the lesson

Directions

1. To bridge between what students already know and the concept of a table and a graph, ask students (or remember if you have taught this lesson), "What is a graph?" You may need to provide them with a definition or elaborate on their ideas (graphs condense data and/or displays numeric information important to the text. They can be used to compare amounts or show changes over time).

2. Show students a table. See example:

Estimated Yearly Cost of Owning a Pet

Costs	Cat	Rabbit	Guinea Pig
Food	$120.00	$110.00	$75.00
Medical	$150.00	$125.00	$50.00
Litter	$150.00	$400.00	$400.00
Toys	$50.00	$25.00	$25.00
Estimated Total Yearly Cost	$470.00	$660.00	$550.00

State, "Tables are used every day. You see them when you read a newspaper or magazine. They are used because they show a lot of information in a small space. A table can help you compare data. Understanding the information in the table allows you to make statements based on the data."

3. Point to the title and say, "The title says 'Estimated Yearly Cost of Owning a Pet.' From this I know that this table will tell me how much it costs per year to own pets." You might want to write the word title or have it pre-written on a sticky note.

4. Say, "I wonder what pets are on the table?" Point to the top row of the table. "Oh, here they are listed across the top row: cat, rabbit, and guinea pig. This table will compare the costs of these pets."

5. Say, "I wonder what costs will be on the table." Point to the first column. "At the top of this column, it says costs. And going down the column it says food, medical (like taking the pet to the veterinarian or doctor), litter (that is where indoor pets go to the bathroom), toys and estimated total yearly cost (this would be how much it would cost to have that kind of pet for a year). So these will be the costs shown in this table."

6. Point to the bottom row, and say, "Wow, the bottom row is really important because it gives the total amount for the cost of each pet. So if I want to know which pet costs the most to own, I would read that row." Moving your finger across the bottom row, say "It looks like a

rabbit is the most expensive pet on our table. Which pet is least expensive?" Call on a student (hopefully they will respond correctly, cat). If needed, point out why.

7. Ask, "What is another question we could answer from reading the table?" Give students some think time. It may be helpful to have them turn and talk to a classmate. Have students share their questions. Write the questions on chart paper or the whiteboard. If needed, assist students in revising questions. Have the other students answer the questions.

8. Close the lesson by reviewing the purpose of a table (they organize and condense data into columns and rows with headings, allowing the reader to compare information and make statements about the data).

Modifications (for younger, less-able, or LEP students)

The visual image will be helpful, but pictures to go with the table are recommended. For example, show the picture of each pet and then pictures of items that could be costs while caring for the animal, such as cat litter.

Assessment Options

Assessment will be done throughout the lesson via observation and by providing students with feedback on the questions they create.

Technology

Display the table on a document camera or an interactive whiteboard.

Purpose

To review what a table and its purpose is, and to learn the parts of a table.

Prerequisite Skills

Students should know what a table is and its purpose is. They should also be familiar with some text features, such as title, captions, and labels. This lesson should be broken into two lessons as described for younger learners. Older learners may be able to complete both parts in one sitting.

Materials

A table, such as the one that is provided with the lesson below (also see *Thinksheet 3.19: African Animal Fun Facts*)

Directions

Part I

1. Review what a table is: "Tables organize and condense data into columns and rows with headings. How does a table help a reader? It allows the reader to compare information and make statements about the data."

2. Depending on the grade level you are using this lesson for, you may want to skip to step 3 in the directions. For grades three and up, we suggest using the following as an introduction: "When reading a table, there are several things we need to pay attention to. These are: the table title, row or column labels, information given in individual cells, information given within rows and columns, and the relationship between rows and columns." Sticky-note labels of the parts of the table would be beneficial if you are not able to project the table for all students to see.

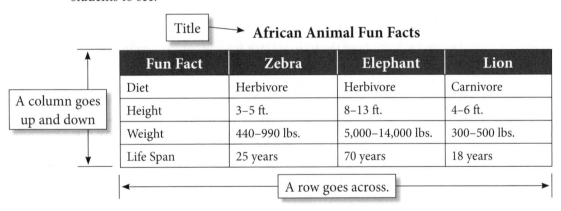

African Animal Fun Facts

Fun Fact	Zebra	Elephant	Lion
Diet	Herbivore	Herbivore	Carnivore
Height	3–5 ft.	8–13 ft.	4–6 ft.
Weight	440–990 lbs.	5,000–14,000 lbs.	300–500 lbs.
Life Span	25 years	70 years	18 years

3. Ask, "What is a title?" Students should be able to tell you that a title explains, or gives an overview of, what you are going to read about. If you have not shown them a table yet, display one such as that above. Ask, "What is the title of this table?" They should be able to point and/ or read the title to you. Then ask, "What does this title tell us about this table?" Correct any responses that are illogical. Add, "The title of a table is always located at the top of the table."

4. Ask, "What type of African animals are on this table?" They should reply: zebra, elephant, and lion. If they have difficulty with this, use a think-aloud and point to the top row of the table. It may be helpful to label what a row is and what a column is.

5. Ask, "What fun facts will we learn about a zebra, elephant and lion?" They should reply: diet, size, weight, and life span. If they have difficulty with this, use a think-aloud and point to the first column labeled "Fun Fact." Then run your finger down the column and read off each type of fact. You may want to explain what each means, such as that a diet is made up of the type of foods someone eats.

6. Say, "Now we can read a cell to find out the details about the specific fun fact we want to know about. For example, if we want to know the life span (how long something usually lives) of an elephant, we would need to find the row in the first column labeled "Life Span" (point to this row with one hand) and then the column labeled "Elephant" (point to this column with the other hand). Where the two meet is where we will have our answer (move both hands until they come together and circle this cell). Then say, "It says 70 years."

Part II

1. Say, "Now, I am going to ask you some questions that are answered on the table. If you think you know the answer, give me a thumbs-up to let me know you are ready (this could be also completed using clickers or polling students with an interactive whiteboard so all students could respond)." Offer corrective feedback as needed.
   a. Is a zebra an herbivore (eats plants) or a carnivore (eats meat)? Herbivore
   b. Which animal is a carnivore? Lion
   c. How much do elephants weigh? Between 5,000–14,000 lbs.
   d. Which animal is three to five feet? Zebra

2. Ask students to make a statement based on the information and data on the table. For example, "A lion is a carnivore." Again provide feedback as needed.

Modifications (for younger, less-able, or LEP students)

For Part II, you could provide sentence frames such as "A lion is a _____." Or, "A lion lives _____ years."

Assessment Options

Assessment should be done throughout the lesson. Have students answer a question that requires them to read the table (see step 6) or complete *Thinksheet 3.20: Reading a Table*. Students could also develop a "How to Read a Table" poster for reference. For example, when reading tables, you should:
1. Read the title to determine the subject of the table.
2. Think about what you might expect to be on the table based on the title.
3. Read across the first row of the table (at the top). What are the columns of the table about?
4. Read down the first column (on the left hand side). What is each row of the table about?
5. How are the things on the first row and the first column related to each other and to the title of the table?

Technology

Display Thinksheet 3.19 on a document camera or an interactive whiteboard. Use an interactive whiteboard with a clicker feature for Part II.

Purpose

To have students create a table.

Prerequisite Skills

Students should know what a table is and the parts of the table you are asking them to include. The rubric can be modified according to your expectations. This would not be appropriate for students in kindergarten or first grade. If the lesson is used in second- and third-grade classes, you will need to provide heavy scaffolding for the creation of a table. It is recommended that at any grade level, you first develop a table together and model the process prior to having students do this independently.

Materials

Thinksheet 3.21: Creating a Table to provide some support to students in the process; *Thinksheet 3.22: Table Rubric* to evaluate students' tables; and *Thinksheet 3.19: African Animal Fun Facts* (or see below)

Directions

1. Review what a table is and the parts of a table. A table organizes and condenses data into columns and rows with headings/labels. A table has a title and labels for each row and each column.
2. Say, "Today you are going to create your own table. For this table you will research your favorite animals and find out fun facts about them. Then you will display your fun facts in a table."
3. Say, "Look at this table. We used this table when we first learned about tables. This table is called 'African Animal Fun Facts.'"

African Animal Fun Facts

Fun Fact	Zebra	Elephant	Lion
Diet	Herbivore	Herbivore	Carnivore
Height	3–5 ft.	8–13 ft.	4–6 ft.
Weight	440–990 lbs.	5,000–14,000 lbs.	300–500 lbs.
Life Span	25 years	70 years	18 years

4. Distribute and display *Thinksheet 3.21*. If needed, use the African Animal Fun Fact table to review the parts of a table. Use a think-aloud to explain what students will do to complete the thinksheet.
5. This activity can be repeated with other topics, such as state facts, capital facts, and country facts.
6. Allow students time to research and then complete *Thinksheet 3.21*. Have them create a final draft of their table.

Modifications (for younger, less-able, or LEP students)

Strategically pair students to create a table.

Assessment Options

Use *Thinksheet 3.22: Table Rubric* to evaluate students' tables.

Technology

Students can do the research for this table online. They can use a word-processing program to create the final draft of their table. Display Thinksheet 3.21 on an interactive whiteboard, or have students work on computers to complete and then print pages.

Chapter 4
Organizational Features Mini-lessons

Overview for Teaching Organizational Features

For students, finding their way around informational texts can be tricky. Since expository texts don't often follow the narrative path of beginning, middle, and end, students are often confused about how to find specific information. Organizational features such as the table of contents, index, and glossary can help students navigate unfamiliar terrain and find what they are looking for before frustration sets in.

It is tempting to treat lessons on these types of features as simple scavenger hunts: "Locate the page where _____ is found." And we have every confidence you can create these types of lessons without any help from us. In the lessons presented here, however, we have chosen to focus more on the kinds of information found in organizational features as well as how to use them. Students who can navigate through a more complicated text will comprehend more and rely less on you for guidance.

The table below lists the features taught in this chapter and the grade level(s) when these features should be mastered.

Figure 6: **Organizational Features End-of-grade-level Expectations and Lessons Related to Each Text Feature**

ORGANIZATIONAL FEATURES End-of-grade-level Expectations and Lessons Related to Each Text Feature	K	1	2	3	4	5
Table of Contents	✗	✗	✗	✗	✗	✗
Where Is It? . . . . p. 99						
Write a Table of Contents . . . . p. 100						
Index		✗	✗	✗	✗	✗
What Is an Index? . . . . p. 101						
Alphabetic Index . . . . p. 102						
Write an Index . . . . p. 103						
Glossary		✗	✗	✗	✗	✗
What Is a Glossary? . . . . p. 105						
What Words Are in a Glossary? . . . . p. 106						
Readers' Theatre Script: What Are Organizational Features?						

Readers' Theatre Script Overview

Once your students have learned most or a good number of the text features in this chapter, you might consider accessing the CD for the readers' theatre script that corresponds to print features. The readers' theatre script can be used as a culminating activity or serve as an enrichment activity for students who excel at text features. You might even have a performance for parents at a family literacy evening or curriculum night.

Materials for Lessons

As you are teaching these text features, it is important to give special consideration to the types of text you use. It is worthwhile to spend the time to find interesting, well-written texts that contain good examples of the feature you are highlighting. We've included a limited bibliography of useful texts in **Appendix D: Suggested Resources for Teaching Text Features** (page 136). You should definitely supplement these with books from your classroom and school library. When the book fair is in town, take a moment to peruse the non-fiction selections. There are many great texts from which to choose. Please also remember that thinksheet lesson companions can be found on the CD.

Organizational Feature Lesson Definitions and Introductions

Table of contents. If someone were looking to take a shortcut on summarizing a non-fiction book, in most cases, she could simply read off the table of contents in the order it is written. Used to help readers locate subtopics of a text by listing chapter titles and page numbers where each begins, the table of contents is often only used by students when they are told to do so. Learning how to use a table of contents to not only find information, but also get acquainted with the main ideas in a text, can be very helpful for children. Writing a table of contents for their own text helps students better organize their work.

Index. We often need to find specific details from the informational texts we read. Whether we are trying to find a recipe for crepes or determine the types of crafts the Seminole Indians made two hundred years ago, it doesn't always help to go through the table of contents. Students given a topic to research and write about can easily be fooled into selecting a text that is only marginally related if they don't use the index to pinpoint the detailed knowledge they want. Students need to know that the index is located at the back of the book, that it contains specific topics with the page numbers where information about the topics can be found, and that the topics are listed in alphabetical order. Teaching students how to use an index gives them the power to focus in on the desired knowledge.

Glossary. Ask any student what she should do when she doesn't know what a word means, and nine out of ten times she will say, "Look it up!" It doesn't make sense to frequently stop reading and look up words, but there are some words that are so important readers must understand them to grasp the main idea. Looking up words in a dictionary is hit or miss for students—they have to sift through multiple meanings and jargon to try and figure out what the word means. Having a glossary—words defined specifically for the text and located right in the back of it—is very helpful. Most authors also have the glossary words highlighted or bolded in the text where they appear to indicate they are important. Thinking of what words to include and writing their own glossaries helps students deepen their understanding of a topic.

Purpose

To help students understand that a table of contents lists chapter titles in the order they appear in the book and tells what page each chapter begins on; to help students use a table of contents to locate topics of interest.

Prerequisite Skills

Students must know that a table of contents lists chapter titles.

Materials

Sample table of contents (see Table 1.2 and CD for one possible example)

Directions

1. Explain, "The table of contents is kind of like a map. It tells you where to find the main topics in a book. Each topic is its own chapter and has a chapter title. The chapter title is what is listed in the table of contents. A table of contents also lists the first page number of each chapter. A table of contents is located in the front of a book before the chapters begin. Today you will be reading a table of contents and figuring out where each chapter begins and ends."
2. Tell students, "The title of this book is *Magnet Power*. Do you know anything about magnets?" Lead a brief discussion about what students already know, and generate a list of topics that might be in this book.
3. Display the sample table of contents on an overhead, interactive whiteboard, or document camera.
4. Read the chapter titles aloud. Say (while pointing to the first chapter title): "The first chapter, 'What Is a Magnet?' begins on page 4. What page does this chapter end on?" Remember to give students some think time. If necessary, prompt by pointing out that the next chapter begins on page 10.
5. Prompt students to find the pages on which various chapters begin and end.
6. Have students explore the table of contents in their own non-fiction trade book or textbook.
7. Repeat this lesson using multiple copies of appropriate books so students can find the chapters both in the table of contents and the actual text.

Modifications (for younger, less-able, or LEP students)

Have students work in small groups and use an example of a table of contents from a set of trade books. Lead students to first find the first page of each chapter in the table of contents and then to find the information in the actual book for confirmation.

Assessment Options

Once students have participated in the lesson and at least one follow-up assessment, it is appropriate to assess informally, either one on one by having them find certain chapters, or through a quiz where you provide a table of contents and have students list the first and last pages of various chapters.

Technology

Use a document camera or an interactive whiteboard to display the table of contents.

Purpose

To help students understand how to create a table of contents.

Prerequisite Skills

Students must know that a table of contents lists chapter titles in the order they appear in the book and tells what page each chapter begins on. They must also be able to identify a chapter title in an age-appropriate non-fiction trade book.

Materials

Age-appropriate non-fiction trade books (preferably one per pair of students) with a piece of construction paper covering the table of contents (paperclips will work and won't damage the book); *Thinksheet 4.1: Write a Table of Contents*

Directions

1. Ask, "What is a table of contents? What information can be found there?" Students should be able to tell you that a table of contents tells the reader where chapters are located. It lists chapter titles in the order they appear and tells where to find the first page of each chapter.
2. Explain that each pair of students will get a book that has a table of contents and chapters. The table of contents has been covered. They are going to use the chapter titles to write their own table of contents.
3. Have students go through and point to each chapter title while you monitor to ensure they can find the chapter titles.
4. Remind students, "The table of contents lists chapter titles in the order they appear, and the page listed by each chapter title is where that chapter begins."
5. Instruct students to write the book's table of contents that they created on *Thinksheet 4.1*.
6. When students finish, help them remove the cover off the actual table of contents so they can check their work.

Modifications (for younger, less-able, or LEP students)

Using a Big Book, work as a group to create the table of contents on chart paper.

Assessment Options

Check to ensure students wrote the chapter titles in order and listed the correct page where each chapter began.

Technology

Using an e-book on an interactive whiteboard, skip the table of contents and have students create a table of contents on a piece of paper on their desks as you flip through the book showing each chapter title. You could also use a shared text and have students create the table of contents on the interactive whiteboard.

Purpose

To help students learn how to use an index to find specific information in the text.

Prerequisite Skills

Students should know the difference between specific and general (or basic) information.

Materials

Age-appropriate trade books with indexes

Directions

1. Begin by telling students that the index is a place in the book where you can find very specific information. It is like a Table of Contents (TOC) because it shows page numbers where information is found. Unlike a TOC, the index can tell you the exact page where something is found, not just the first page of a chapter. It can help you see if the book has information you are looking for. The index is located at the back of a book.
2. Give each pair of students a trade book and ask them to find the index. Coach as needed.
3. Show students the following index either copied on chart paper, on a worksheet, or on the projection screen.

Index	
attracts	8, 13
compass	20
Earth(s)	16, 18, 20
magnetic field	6, 8, 16, 20
pole(s)	10, 12, 13, 14, 16, 17, 18
repel	14

4. Ask them to tell you on which page they would find information on a compass, magnetic field, etc. Tell them that when more than one page is shown, the information can be found on all the pages listed.
5. Ask students what type of information they notice in the index: Is the author's name listed here? Are there illustrations? Definitions of words? Does it tell where chapters begin?
6. Ask what the topic of this book might be.
7. Remind students that an index is found at the back of a book and lists pages where you can find specific information.

Modifications (for younger, less-able, or LEP students)

- Work in a small group so you can monitor work more easily.
- Repeat the lesson using different trade books to ensure students understand the concepts associated with indexes.

Assessment Options

Ask questions to assess understanding. Because this is the first lesson, it is not appropriate to assess mastery.

Technology

Use a projection device to show the example index, or show indexes from e-books.

Purpose

To help students find specific information in the index.

Prerequisite Skills

Students should know alphabetical order and the difference between specific and general (or basic) information.

Materials

Thinksheet 4.2: Alphabetical Index Sorting Cards

Directions

1. Review that an index is a place in the book where you can find very specific information. It is like a Table of Contents (TOC) because it shows page numbers where information is found. Unlike a TOC, the index can tell you the exact page where something is found, not just the first page of where a chapter can be found. It can help you see if the book has information you are looking for. The index is located at the back of a book.
2. Show students the following example of an index and ask them to notice how the information is organized.

Index	
attracts	8, 13
compass	20
Earth(s)	16, 18, 20
magnetic field	6, 8, 16, 20
pole(s)	10, 12, 13, 14, 16, 17, 18
repel	14

3. If students don't pick up on it, point out that it is organized in alphabetical order. Tell them that authors organize a table of contents in alphabetical order so readers can find what they are looking for more easily.
4. If necessary, review how to alphabetize by first letter.
5. Hand out the index order sort cards (*Thinksheet 4.2*), and instruct students to work with a partner to sort cards in alphabetical order. (Key: brakes, chain, helmet, mountain bike, road bike, safety, tricycle, wheels)
6. When students have finished, go over the correct order. Ask students, "If you had a card with the topic of *accessories* on it, where would it go?" Answer: before brakes.
7. "What would you expect a book to be about if it had these things in the index?" Possible answers: bicycles, bike safety.

Modifications (for younger, less-able, or LEP students)

- Work together to alphabetize.
- Include pictures on cards.

Assessment Options

As students sort through the cards, observe them and ensure they understand how to put the cards in alphabetical order.

Technology

Use a projection device to show the example index.

Purpose

To help students understand what types of information can be found in an index and how to create an index for their own writing.

Prerequisite Skills

Students should know alphabetical order and the difference between specific and general (or basic) information. Students should understand the concept of a topic.

Materials

Thinksheet 4.3: Create an Index

Directions

1. Review what an index is and how it is organized.
2. Tell students that today they will be creating an index of a book that is about school.
3. Brainstorm a list of general topics to be included in a book on school. Examples might be supplies, classes, and people.
4. Record the list laterally with each broad topic written so it can be the heading of a column.

   Example

<u>Supplies</u>	<u>Classes</u>	<u>People</u>

5. Next, brainstorm more specific details that might be included under each heading. For example, under the heading "Supplies," you might list pencils, crayons, books, glue, and paper.
6. Tell students to imagine that they have written this book already and that now they have been asked to create an index for the book. On *Thinksheet 4.3: Create an Index,* have students write the topics and subtopics they feel would be in the index. Have the more advanced students think about how these topics might be organized in a book and put approximate page numbers on their indexes. For example, they might list the same pages for pencil, paper, rulers and crayons after assuming these things would be on a page about school supplies.

Modifications (for younger, less-able, or LEP students)

Place students who need more support in small groups.

Assessment Options

Because the index should be organized in alphabetical order rather than the order the items appear in, watch to ensure that students who completed the more advanced activity with page numbers do not list the numbers in order.

Technology

The brainstormed list and *Thinksheet 4.3* can be completed on an interactive whiteboard or on individual computers.

Thinksheet 4.3: Create an Index   Name: _____

Index

Topic	Page numbers
_____	_____
_____	_____
_____	_____
_____	_____
_____	_____
_____	_____
_____	_____
_____	_____
_____	_____

Purpose

To help students know what type of information can be found in a glossary and where a glossary is located.

Prerequisite Skills

Students must be familiar with partner work and willing to search for answers.

Materials

Samples of student books, such as textbooks and non-fiction trade books that have glossaries (at least three per pair of students); *Thinksheet 4.4: What Is a Glossary?* (one per group)

Directions

1. Tell students that glossaries are a special part of many informational books. Today, students are going to find glossaries and look at them to figure out what kind of information they contain.
2. Instruct students to work in pairs and to find and then bookmark the glossary in each of the texts they are found in.
3. As they do this, have them complete the table on *Thinksheet 4.4: What Is a Glossary?* Go over the directions for completing the table before students begin.
4. As students are working, observe to ensure they are able to find the glossaries. Ask probing questions to help them know what type of information to include in the last column of the thinksheet. Ask questions such as, "Does this section tell you where to find information? What does it do?"
5. After each group is finished, pull the class together, and tell students they will all share their data so they can learn about glossaries. Ask students to share where they found each glossary, and ask them where they think they should look if they are reading a book and want to find the glossary. They should tell you they would look near the end of the text.
6. Ask students about the type of information they found in the glossaries. They should tell you that glossaries give the meanings of words. Ask students if glossaries give the meanings of all the words we read and write. Follow up by asking why the words were included in the glossary. If they don't come up with it themselves, tell students that a glossary helps readers understand what the important and new words in a text mean.

Modifications (for younger, less-able, or LEP students)

This is an inquiry-based lesson. You may make the decision to tell some students where to find the glossary and what type of information they will find there. Then, you can use the same text and have students complete the thinksheet as a group.

Assessment Options

Ask students to tell you where they would find a glossary and what kind of information would be found in one.

Technology

Use the projector to complete the thinksheet and examples of text.

Purpose

To help students understand what types of words can be found in a glossary, determine what words are important to a text, and determine how words are organized in a glossary.

Prerequisite Skills

Students must understand that a glossary gives definitions of words in a text.

Materials

Enough copies of trade books or textbooks that include glossaries with bolded or highlighted words so that each student can look at an example or an e-book on the projector

Directions

1. Ask students what a glossary is. They should be able to tell you that a glossary is a section at the back of an informational text that gives you the definition of words. Ask them if a glossary defines all the words people speak and read. They should tell you that it only give certain words.
2. Tell students that authors select words important for readers to understand from the main body of the text, and they include them in the glossary. Glossary words are often new to the reader. Readers can look up words in a glossary to help them understand the text better. Usually, words that are defined in the glossary are shown in bold or highlighted in the main body of the text.
3. Show the example below (from *Magnet Power*, Rourke Educational Publishing, page 8) on a projector, doc cam, or overhead, and ask student to notice which word is bold. Next, show the glossary for this book (page 23) and ask students to notice the same word. Point out that the words in the glossary are listed alphabetically to make them easier for readers to find.
4. Have students look at their sample texts and find a bold or highlighted word. Next, have them look in the glossary to see if the word is there. You can have them repeat this several times.
5. Have students share what they found. (Findings should include words in the glossary that are in bolded or highlighted in the text.)
6. Show the glossary from the book *Magnet Power* again. Help students read the words and definitions and ask, "Why would these words be in a book named *Magnet Power*?" Hopefully, they will say, "Because you need to understand these words to understand magnets." If students don't respond with a similar answer, tell them that this is the case.

Modifications (for younger, less-able, or LEP students)

Use a lower-level text that still includes a glossary. Use a picture glossary. Work in small groups.

Assessment Options

Observe to find students who know where to find the glossary.

Technology

Use the projector, document camera, or overhead projector to show the materials from *Magnet Power*.

> **Glossary**
>
> **attracts** (uh-TRAKTS): pulls toward
> **force** (FORS): something that pulls or pushes something else
> **magnet** (MAG-nit): an object that attracts iron and has a magnetic field
> **magnetic field** (mag-NEH-tik FEELD): area around a magnet with the power to attract iron
> **poles** (POLES): the two opposite ends of a magnet
> **repel** (rih-P[

> All magnets have a magnetic field. The field **attracts** iron, nickel, and certain other metals.

Chapter 5
Integrating and Showing Text Feature Knowledge

Sometimes you have to pull something apart and fix the pieces to get it working right. That's just what we have done in the previous chapters when it comes to teaching text features. But knowledge of individual text features is just one part of comprehending informational text. We need to put those pieces back together again and coordinate all the parts to aid comprehension even further. Ultimately, we want students to be able to pick up any text and know how to extract the full meaning.

In this chapter, we highlight some extra activities you can do when teaching any text feature. We'll also introduce structures that will lend themselves to having students use their knowledge of multiple features. The goal of these activities is to reinforce the lessons you have taught and encourage students to integrate their text feature knowledge. Many activities also provide an opportunity to showcase student learning.

We end with explicit directions for pulling all this learning together in a very powerful structure, the text feature walk. Picture your students working in groups, previewing and discussing all of the text features in a piece of text, sharing background knowledge, asking questions about the text, and predicting what will be read. Such is a typical description of students who know text features and how to use them to their full advantage.

Text Feature Matching and Sorting Activities

Matching and sorting activities can be very engaging for students. You can cut out images and text on *Thinksheets 5.1–5.3* on the CD to have students sort or match the following:

- Text feature examples to text feature names
- Text feature names to text feature definitions
- Text feature examples to text feature definitions

Text features can be removed from the matching and sorting depending upon what your expectations are, the grade level that you are teaching, and what you have taught.

Text Feature Scavenger Hunt

This activity allows students to practice identifying specific text features or to show identification mastery. Once students have been taught a text feature, ask them to hunt through their guided-reading book, textbooks, or pre-selected trade books and find examples of one or more specific text features. From here, the text features can be recorded or noted in different ways. You can have students record text features found on a T-chart (see *Thinksheet 5.4* on the CD), with the name of the text feature being listed on the left side and the page number where they found the text feature listed on the right side of the "T." Another option is to have students place a sticky note on the text feature in the book and write the name of the text feature on the sticky note. This way, when you meet with them in small groups, you can go through the text together and have students share text features and where they found them. With older students, you may consider using a matrix. We have included matrixes for students to record where they found the feature for each of the chapters in this text: print, graphic, and organizational (see *Thinksheets 5.5–5.7* in the book and on the CD). We have also included a blank matrix that allows you to put in the specific text features you want students to find (*Thinksheet 5.8*), features you have taught, and/or features you expect students to know.

Morning Message Opportunity

Abraham Lincoln was born today. He was our sixteenth president. He liked to read. He lived in a cabin. He lived in the state of Kentucky. He helped make rules and laws. He was loved.

One day, when visiting Sharon Smith's kindergarten classroom, this message was posted on the board as students settled in for their day. The teacher called all of the students together and shared the morning message with her students. Then she had the students chorally read the text with her. When she finished, she said, "Something is missing from our morning message. Does anyone know what might be missing?" A student quickly responded with "A title." The teacher then prompted students to come up with a good title for the morning message. She wrote all of the students' ideas on the board. Some of their titles were "President's Day," "Lincoln's Birthday," and "Abraham Lincoln." Although all of these titles were relevant, the teacher explained that one title was the best because it was about the entire passage rather than just one part. She used think-aloud to talk about each title in relationship to the topic of the message. She then wrote "Abraham Lincoln" at the top of the morning message.

This took less than ten minutes, but what a great opportunity to practice and reinforce knowledge of the title text feature! This could be done with many different text features. You could even have students create or suggest a text feature to go with the morning message. For example, ask students to come up with a good photograph or drawing to go with the morning message above. Think about the possibilities, even with older students. Imagine posting a graph with the axis not labeled or a diagram missing a title and having students come up with the missing information.

Text Feature Flap Books

Flap books are not only fun to create, but they are also a good reference tool for students. Identify which text features are most commonly found in the content text you use, and have students create a flap book with those text features. Alternatively, have students create a flap book organized by the categories of text features you have taught: print, graphic, and organizational.

Flap book directions. See the following directions and photos for creating a flap book.

1. Have students fold paper in half lengthwise and crease it.
2. On one side of the folded paper, cut slits on the front flap only, from the open edge up to the fold. Determine the number of flaps according to how many text features you want the students to demonstrate.
3. On the front of each flap, have students write the name of the text feature.
4. On the inside of each flap, have students write the definition for the text feature.
5. Under each flap, have students draw or find an example of the text feature from a newspaper or discarded magazine.

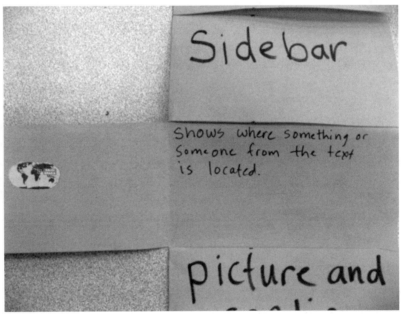
Inside of flap book

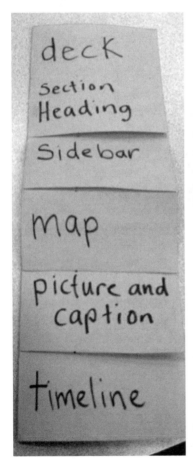
Outside of flap book

Class Text Feature Wall
(Kelley & Clausen-Grace, 2007)

The class text feature wall is a collaborative and interactive project. Students find examples of the different text features they have been learning about and then cut and paste these onto a class text feature wall. The wall can be a work in progress that gets added to as you teach and students learn new text features.

Text Feature Folder

If your classroom does not have space for a text feature wall, you might have students create their own mini-version as a text feature folder. Have students add text features to a manila folder as they learn them. Students can draw, tape, and/or paste on a text feature example and label it. With older students, you may want them to also include a definition for the text feature. This could be a folder that is completed throughout the school year as students learn new text features. It can also serve as a reminder or a reference when needed.

"How to Read a _____" Poster or Book

Students can make a "How to Read" poster or book for any of the text features you are learning about or for commonly read texts, such as student periodicals. Many of the graphic features lessons in this book have directions that guide students in how to read a specific text feature. The content in these lessons could be used by students to develop a "How to Read" poster or book.

Begin by selecting a focus for the book. If you are using a student periodical or textbook, make sure all students have access to a copy or two. This activity is especially helpful if you use a text that you will be using for instruction throughout the year. Ask students to look at the headings for each page and see if these are recurring sections. In the following example, students are explaining one of the recurring columns in *Weekly Reader* called "News Debate."

Choose one section to focus on at a time. Have students come up with a list of the features of this section and then share what they have noticed as a whole group. Keep track of all the features the students noticed on a piece of chart paper. Discuss and record the function of each text feature on your chart. For example, in the picture below, the students identified the heading and wrote that it tells what the article is about. You would record this on the chart so students can reference it when creating their book page or poster.

Next, have students glue the actual page (if it is a student periodical) or a scanned copy on a piece of larger paper, making sure to keep enough room in the margins to write. Students then label each text feature and describe what it does. Make sure students include features that are specific to the particular text you are using.

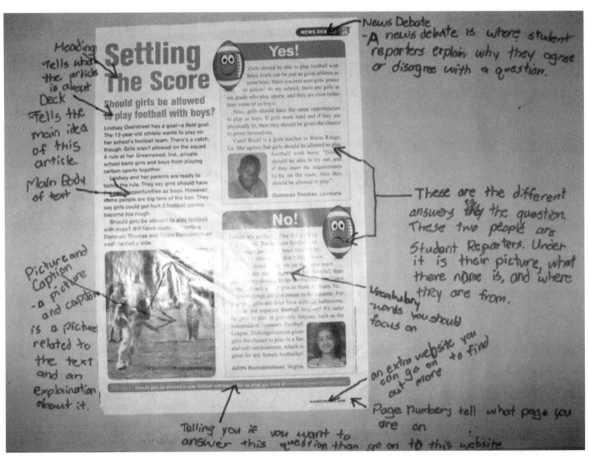

Page from a student-created "How to Read a Weekly Reader" book

Class Book of _____

Once students have learned how to read and write a specific text feature, you can make a class book of features. For example, after learning about pictures (photographs and drawings) with captions, students can create a "Class Book of Pictures with Captions." Each student can take a photograph or draw a picture and write a caption to go with the picture, creating his or her own page in the class book. Or, depending upon the grade level you are working with, you could assign students partners and the page could be shared. You can easily tie this to content by giving the book a theme. For example, you might create a class book about your school.

Text Feature Interview

The text feature interview is a fun, effective way to help students read a variety of text features and put the information together to help front-load vocabulary and concepts for a text to be read. To prepare, you need to photocopy and cut out all the text features from a section of text. Glue individual features to the center of separate sheets of copy paper. Give each student a text feature and two sticky notes. Tell students they are going to be reading each other's text features in order to accurately predict what an upcoming section of text is about. The first step is to have students read the text feature pasted on their paper. On one of the sticky notes, they write down what their text feature is (name it) and then a prediction of what they think they will be learning about based on their reading of a text feature. The second step is to have students walk about the room and find someone to interview. They ask a classmate what text feature he or she has and what he or she predicts about the reading based on that text feature. Basically, the students are sharing what they wrote on their sticky notes. On their second sticky note, they are gathering what they learn from other classmates and their text features. See the following example for how this looks.

Student's text feature from textbook

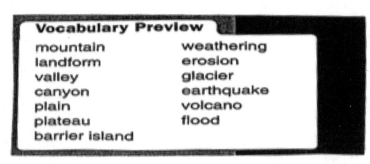

Step 1: Student's initial prediction

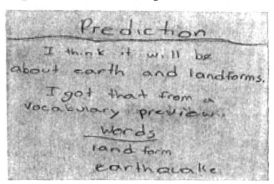

Step 2: Student's interview partners

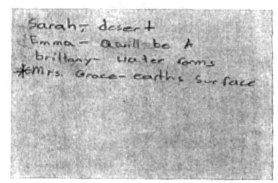

A follow-up class discussion will help bring everyone's ideas together and allow them to formulate a final prediction of what they will be learning. This can be formalized by asking students to revise or broaden their initial predictions, or you could even have students write a predictive summary. After students read the text, have them revisit their predictions and confirm or reject them.

Text Feature Walk

A text feature walk (TFW) is our version of the primary picture walk but kicked up a notch. Picture walks are usually done with narrative early readers and the purpose is to have students predict what they are going to read about. As picture supports diminish, so does the picture walk. Interestingly though, as narrative text loses pictures, informational text gains them in the form of text features.

The TFW (2007, 2008, 2010) is a powerful structure that can be employed once students have had some direct instruction on text features. Depending on what text you want students to walk through, students do not necessarily need to know all text features in order to use the TFW. A quick preview of the text will let you know what types of text features are prevalent and whether your students would have some background knowledge of the these as well as the topic(s) in the text.

During a TFW, students are strategically grouped and asked to preview the text they will be reading. Start by going over how to pronounce any words students may have trouble with so they don't repeatedly mispronounce important vocabulary. Tell them to take turns reading each text feature in the order it occurs. After one student reads the text feature, he and the others in the group predict, question, or connect to the ideas in the text feature. The goal is to have students anticipate what the main idea of the text is going to be and how the text feature relates to this main idea. Once students have "walked" the text, they should have a good idea of what they will be reading and learning about as they read.

With really young students, you will be the facilitator and guide students through the TFW in either a whole or small group. You can expect older students to be able to work in cooperative groups after you have scaffolded, coached, and modeled this structure. It is important to ensure that all groups understand the purpose of the walk: to read the text features and predict, question, and share background knowledge about the main body of text.

Suggestions for TFW success. We have been using this structure for many years with great success, so we have identified some tips to help you in your classroom.

- Use a text that you know students will have some background information on.
- Make sure the text is not too challenging and not too lengthy.
- Identify tricky vocabulary words—those words in the text that you think students may know but may offer a challenge.
- Pronounce and make public the tricky words you identified. If needed, help students make connections to these words or even offer some background information.
- Articulate the goals and process of the TFW.
- Before having students do a TFW in small groups, guide students as a whole class through the process by modeling and thinking aloud as you "walk" through the text features.
- Observe students trying out the TFW, and offer coaching and feedback
- Strategically partner students so that groups have mixed abilities and varied strengths.

Student guide for a TFW. The following directions will help students successfully complete a TFW.

1. Read the title and predict the main idea of the text. Discuss this as a group.

2. Take turns reading each text feature in the order it appears in the text. As you encounter a feature, the person reading it should share his or her prediction, question, or background knowledge of the feature. All others in the group should join in and have a conversation about the feature. Try to figure out how this feature is related to the main idea.

3. After you have read and discussed each feature, work together to come up with a prediction about what the main body of text is.

Appendix A
References

Barton, M.L. (1997). Addressing the literacy crisis: Teaching reading in the content areas. *NASSP Bulletin, 81*(587), 22–30.

Bryce, N. (2011). Meeting the reading challenges of science textbooks in the primary grades. *The Reading Teacher, 64*(7), 474–485.

Clay, M.M. (2000). Concepts about print: What have children learned about the way we use print language? Portsmouth, NH: Heinemann.

Duke, N.K. (2003). Informational text? The research says, "Yes!" In L. Hoyt, M. Mooney, & B. Parkes (Eds.), *Exploring Information Texts: From Theory to Practice* (pp. 2–25). Portsmouth, NH: Heinemann.

Hannus, M., & Hyona, J. (1999). Utilization of illustrations during learning of science textbook passages among low- and high-ability children. *Contemporary Educational Psychology, 24(2),* 95–123.

Kelley, M. & Clausen-Grace, N. (2010). Using a text feature walk to purposefully guide students through expository text. *The Reading Teacher, 64 (3),* 191–195.

Kelley, M. & Clausen-Grace, N. (2008). From picture walk to text feature walk: Guiding students to strategically preview text. *Journal of Content Area Reading, 7(1),* 9–32.

Kelley, M. & Clausen-Grace, N. (2007). *Comprehension shouldn't be silent: From strategy instruction to student independence.* Newark, DE: International Reading Association.

McTigue, E.M. & Flowers, A.C. (2011). Science visual literacy: Learners' perceptions and knowledge of diagrams. *The Reading Teacher, 64(8),* 578–589.

Pearson, P.D., & Gallagher, M.C. (1983). The instruction of reading comprehension. Contemporary Educational Psychology, 8, 317–344.

Yeh, Y.Y. & McTigue, E.M. (2009). The frequency, variation, and function of graphical representations within standardized state science tests. *School Science and Mathematics, 109(8),* 435–449.

Appendix B
Common Core Reading Standards Relevant to Teaching Children to Read

Table 1.1: **K-5 Common Core Reading Standards Relevant to Teaching Children to Read, Understand, and Use Text Features across the Curriculum**

Common Core	Grade K	Grade 1	Grade 2	Grade 3	Grade 4	Grade 5
			Informational Text (RI) Standards			
Key Ideas and Details	1. With prompting and support, ask and answer questions about key details in a text.	Ask and answer questions about key details in a text.	Ask and answer such questions as *who, what, where, when, why,* and *how* to demonstrate understanding of key details in a text.	Ask and answer questions to demonstrate under-standing of a text, referring explicitly to the text as the basis for the answers.	Refer to details and examples in a text when explaining what the text says explicitly and when drawing inferences from the text.	Quote accurately from a text when explaining what the text says explicitly and when drawing inferences from the text.
Key Ideas and Details	2. With prompting and support, identify the main topic and retell key details of a text.	Identify the main topic and retell key details of a text.	Identify the main topic of a multi-paragraph text as well as the focus of specific paragraphs within the text.	Determine the main idea of a text; recount the key details and explain how they support the main idea.	Determine the main idea of a text and explain how it is supported by key details; summarize the text.	Determine two or more main ideas of a text and explain how they are supported by key details summarize the text.
Key Ideas and Details	3. With prompting and support, describe the connection between two individuals, events, ideas, or pieces of information in a text.	Describe the connection between two individuals, events, ideas, or pieces of information in a text.	Describe the connection between a series of historical events, scientific ideas or concepts, or steps in technical procedures in a text.	Describe the relationship between a series of historical events, scientific ideas or concepts, or steps in technical procedures in a text, using language that pertains to time, sequence, and cause/effect.	Explain events, procedures, ideas, or concepts in a historical, scientific, or technical text, including what happened and why, based on specific informa-tion in the text.	Explain the relationships or interactions between two or more individuals, events, ideas, or concepts in a historical, scientific, or technical text based on specific information in the text.
Craft and Structure	4. With prompting and support, ask and answer questions about unknown words in a text.	Ask and answer questions to help determine or clarify the meaning of words and phrases in a text.	Determine the meaning of words and phrases in a text relevant to a *grade 2 topic or subject area.*	Determine the meaning of general academic and domain-specific words and phrases in a text relevant to a *grade 3 topic or subject area.*	Determine the meaning of general academic and domain-specific words or phrases in a text relevant to a *grade 4 topic or subject area.*	Determine the meaning of general academic and domain-specific words and phrases in a text relevant to a *grade 5 topic or subject area.*
Craft and Structure	5. Identify the front cover, back cover, and title page of a book.	Know and use various text features (e.g., headings, tables of contents, glos-saries, electronic menus, icons) to locate key facts or information in a text.	Know and use various text features (e.g., captions, bold print, subheadings, glos-saries, indexes, electronic menus, icons) to locate key facts or information in a text efficiently.	Use text features and search tools (e.g., key words, side-bars, hyperlinks) to locate information relevant to a given topic efficiently.	Describe the overall struc-ture (e.g., chronology, comparison, cause/effect, problem/solution) of events, ideas, concepts, or information in a text or part of a text.	Compare and contrast the overall structure (e.g., chronology, comparison, cause/effect, problem/ solution) of events, ideas, concepts, or information in two or more texts.

Continued

Table 1.1: K–5 Common Core Reading Standards Relevant to Teaching Children to Read, Understand, and Use Text Features across the Curriculum (continued)

Common Core	Grade K	Grade 1	Grade 2	Grade 3	Grade 4	Grade 5
Craft and Structure	6. Name the author and illustrator of a text and define the role of each in presenting the ideas or information in a text.	Distinguish between information provided by pictures or other illustrations and information provided by the words in a text.	Identify the main purpose of a text, including what the author wants to answer, explain, or describe.	Distinguish their own point of view from that of the author of a text.	Compare and contrast a firsthand and secondhand account of the same event or topic; describe the differences in focus and the information provided.	Analyze multiple accounts of the same event or topic, noting important similarities and differences in the point of view they represent.
Integration of Knowledge and Ideas	7. With prompting and support, describe the relationship between illustrations and the text in which they appear (e.g., what person, place, thing, or idea in the text an illustration depicts).	Use the illustrations and details in a text to describe its key ideas.	Explain how specific images (e.g., a diagram showing how a machine works) contribute to and clarify a text.	Use information gained from illustrations (e.g., maps, photographs) and the words in a text to demonstrate understanding of the text (e.g., where, when, why, and how key events occur).	Interpret information presented visually, orally, or quantitatively (e.g., in charts, graphs, diagrams, time lines, animations, or interactive elements on Web pages) and explain how the information contributes to an understanding of the text in which it appears.	Draw on information from multiple print or digital sources, demonstrating the ability to locate an answer to a question quickly or to solve a problem efficiently.
Integration of Knowledge and Ideas	8. With prompting and support, identify the reasons an author gives to support points in a text.	Identify the reasons an author gives to support points in a text.	Describe how reasons support specific points the author makes in a text.	Describe the logical connection between particular sentences and paragraphs in a text (e.g., comparison, cause/effect, first/second/third in a sequence).	Explain how an author uses reasons and evidence to support particular points in a text.	Explain how an author uses reasons and evidence to support particular points in a text, identifying which reasons and evidence support which point(s).
Integration of Knowledge and Ideas	9. With prompting and support, identify basic similarities in and differences between two texts on the same topic (e.g., in illustrations, descriptions, or procedures).	Identify basic similarities in and differences between two texts on the same topic (e.g., in illustrations, descriptions, or procedures).	Compare and contrast the most important points presented by two texts on the same topic.	Compare and contrast the most important points and key details presented in two texts on the same topic.	Integrate information from two texts on the same topic in order to write or speak about the subject knowledgeably.	Integrate information from several texts on the same topic in order to write or speak about the subject knowledgeably.
Range of Reading and Level of Text Complexity	10. Actively engage in group reading activities with purpose and understanding.	With prompting and support, read informational texts appropriately complex for grade 1.	By the end of year, read and comprehend informational texts, including history/social studies, science, and technical texts, in the grades 2–3 text complexity band proficiently, with scaffolding as needed at the high end of the range.	By the end of the year, read and comprehend informational texts, including history/social studies, science, and technical texts, at the high end of the grades 2–3 text complexity band independently and proficiently.	By the end of year, read and comprehend informational texts, including history/social studies, science, and technical texts, in the grades 4–5 text complexity band proficiently, with scaffolding as needed at the high end of the range.	By the end of the year, read and comprehend informational texts, including history/social studies, science, and technical texts, at the high end of the grades 4–5 text complexity band independently and proficiently.

Continued

Table 1.1: **K-5 Common Core Reading Standards Relevant to Teaching Children to Read, Understand, and Use Text Features across the Curriculum (*continued*)**

Common Core	Grade K	Grade I	Grade 2	Grade 3	Grade 4	Grade 5
			Speaking and Listening (SL) Standards			
Comprehension and Collaboration	1. Participate in collaborative conversations with diverse partners about *kindergarten topics and texts* with peers and adults in small and larger groups. a. Follow agreed-upon rules for discussions (e.g., listening to others and taking turns speaking about the topics and texts under discussion). b. Continue a conversation through multiple exchanges.	Participate in collaborative conversations with diverse partners about *grade 1 topics and texts* with peers and adults in small and larger groups. a. Follow agreed-upon rules for discussions (e.g., listening to others with care, speaking one at a time about the topics and texts under discussion). b. Build on others' talk in conversations by responding to the comments of others through multiple exchanges. c. Ask questions to clear up any confusion about the topics and texts under discussion.	Participate in collaborative conversations with diverse partners about *grade 2 topics and texts* with peers and adults in small and larger groups. a. Follow agreed-upon rules for discussions (e.g., gaining the floor in respectful ways, listening to others with care, speaking one at a time about the topics and texts under discussion). b. Build on others' talk in conversations by linking their comments to the remarks of others. c. Ask for clarification and further explanation as needed about the topics and texts under discussion.	Engage effectively in a range of collaborative discussions (one-on-one, in groups, and teacher led) with diverse partners on *grade 3 topics and texts*, building on others' ideas and expressing their own clearly. a. Come to discussions prepared, having read or studied required material; explicitly draw on that preparation and other information known about the topic to explore ideas under discussion. b. Follow agreed-upon rules for discussions (e.g., gaining the floor in respectful ways, listening to others with care, speaking one at a time about the topics and texts under discussion). c. Ask questions to check understanding of information presented, stay on topic, and link their comments to the remarks of others. d. Explain their own ideas and understanding in light of the discussion.	Engage effectively in a range of collaborative discussions (one-on-one, in groups, and teacher led) with diverse partners on *grade 4 topics and texts*, building on others' ideas and expressing their own clearly. a. Come to discussions prepared, having read or studied required material; explicitly draw on that preparation and other information known about the topic to explore ideas under discussion. b. Follow agreed-upon rules for discussions and carry out assigned roles. c. Pose and respond to specific questions to clarify or follow up on information, and make comments that contribute to the discussion and link to the remarks of others. d. Review the key ideas expressed and explain their own ideas and understanding in light of the discussion.	Engage effectively in a range of collaborative discussions (one-on-one, in groups, and teacher led) with diverse partners on *grade 5 topics and texts*, building on others' ideas and expressing their own clearly. a. Come to discussions prepared, having read or studied required material; explicitly draw on that preparation and other information known about the topic to explore ideas under discussion. b. Follow agreed-upon rules for discussions and carry out assigned roles. c. Pose and respond to specific questions by making comments that contribute to the discussion and elaborate on the remarks of others. d. Review the key ideas expressed and draw conclusions in light of information and knowledge gained from the discussions.

Continued

Table 1.1: K-5 Common Core Reading Standards Relevant to Teaching Children to Read, Understand, and Use Text Features across the Curriculum (*continued*)

Common Core	Grade K	Grade 1	Grade 2	Grade 3	Grade 4	Grade 5
Comprehension and Collaboration	2. Confirm understanding of a text read aloud or information presented orally or through other media by asking and answering questions about key details and requesting clarification if something is not understood.	Ask and answer questions about key details in a text read aloud or information presented orally or through other media.	Recount or describe key ideas or details from a text read aloud or information presented orally or through other media.	Determine the main ideas and supporting details of a text read aloud or information presented in diverse media and formats, including visually, quantitatively, and orally.	Paraphrase portions of a text read aloud or information presented in diverse media and formats, including visually, quantitatively, and orally.	Summarize a written text read aloud or information presented in diverse media and formats, including, visually, quantitatively, and orally.
Comprehension and Collaboration	3. Ask and answer questions in order to seek help, get information, or clarify something that is not understood.	Ask and answer questions about what a speaker says in order to gather additional information or clarify something that is not understood.	Ask and answer questions about what a speaker says in order to clarify comprehension, gather additional information, or deepen understanding of a topic or issue.	Ask and answer questions about information from a speaker, offering appropriate elaboration and detail.	Identify the reasons and evidence a speaker provides to support particular points.	Summarize the points a speaker makes and explain how each claim is supported by reasons and evidence.
Presentation of Knowledge and Ideas	4. Describe familiar people, places, things, and events and, with prompting and support, provide additional detail.	Describe people, places, things, and events with relevant details, expressing ideas and feelings clearly.	Tell a story or recount an experience with appropriate facts and relevant, descriptive details, speaking audibly in coherent sentences.	Report on a topic or text, tell a story, or recount an experience with appropriate facts and relevant, descriptive details, speaking clearly at an understandable pace	Report on a topic or text, tell a story, or recount an experience in an organized manner, using appropriate facts and relevant, descriptive details to support main ideas or themes; speak clearly at an understandable pace.	Report on a topic or text or present an opinion, sequencing ideas logically and using appropriate facts and relevant, descriptive details to support main ideas or themes; speak clearly at an understandable pace.
Presentation of Knowledge and Ideas	5. Add drawings or other visual displays to descriptions as desired to provide additional detail.	Add drawings or other visual displays to descriptions when appropriate to clarify ideas, thoughts, and feelings.	Create audio recordings of stories or poems; add drawings or other visual displays to stories or recounts of experiences when appropriate to clarify ideas, thoughts, and feelings.	Create engaging audio recordings of stories or poems that demonstrate fluid reading at an understandable pace; add visual displays when appropriate to emphasize or enhance certain facts or details.	Add audio recordings and visual displays to presentations when appropriate to enhance the development of main ideas or themes.	Include multimedia components (e.g., graphics, sound) and visual displays in presentations when appropriate to enhance the development of main ideas or themes.
Presentation of Knowledge and Ideas	6. Speak audibly and express thoughts, feelings, and ideas clearly.	Produce complete sentences when appropriate to task and situation.	Produce complete sentences when appropriate to task and situation in order to provide requested detail or clarification.	Speak in complete sentences when appropriate to task and situation in order to provide requested detail or clarification.	Differentiate between contexts that call for formal English (e.g., presenting ideas) and situations where informal discourse is appropriate (e.g., small-group discussion); use formal English when appropriate to task and situation.	Adapt speech to a variety of contexts and tasks, using formal English when appropriate to task and situation.

Continued

Table 1.1: K-5 Common Core Reading Standards Relevant to Teaching Children to Read, Understand, and Use Text Features across the Curriculum (*continued*)

Common Core	Grade K	Grade 1	Grade 2	Grade 3	Grade 4	Grade 5
			Language (L) Standards			
Vocabulary Acquisition and Use	4. Determine or clarify the meaning of unknown and multiple-meaning words and phrases based on *kindergarten reading and content.* a. Identify new meanings for familiar words and apply them accurately (e.g., knowing *duck* is a bird and learning the verb *to duck*). b. Use the most frequently occurring inflections and affixes (e.g., *-ed, pre-, -ful, -less*) as a clue to the meaning of an unknown word.	Determine or clarify the meaning of unknown and multiple-meaning words and phrases based on *grade 1 reading and content,* choosing flexibly from an array of strategies. a. Use sentence-level context as a clue to the meaning of a word or phrase. b. Use frequently occurring affixes as a clue to the meaning of a word. c. Identify frequently occurring root words (e.g., *look*) and their inflectional forms (e.g., *looks, looked, looking*).	Determine or clarify the meaning of unknown and multiple-meaning words and phrases based on *grade 2 reading and content,* choosing flexibly from an array of strategies. a. Use sentence-level context as a clue to the meaning of a word or phrase. b. Determine the meaning of the new word formed when a known prefix is added to a known word (e.g., *happy/unhappy, tell/retell*). c. Use a known root word as a clue to the meaning of an unknown word with the same root (e.g., *addition, additional*). d. Use knowledge of the meaning of individual words to predict the meaning of compound words (e.g., *birdhouse, lighthouse, housefly; bookshelf, notebook, bookmark*). e. Use glossaries and beginning dictionaries, both print and digital, to determine or clarify the meaning of words and phrases.	Determine or clarify the meaning of unknown and multiple-meaning word and phrases based on *grade 3 reading and content,* choosing flexibly from a range of strategies. a. Use sentence-level context as a clue to the meaning of a word or phrase. b. Determine the meaning of the new word formed when a known affix is added to a known word (e.g., *agreeable/disagreeable, comfortable/uncomfortable, care/careless, heat/preheat*). c. Use a known root word as a clue to the meaning of an unknown word with the same root (e.g., *company, companion*). d. Use glossaries or beginning dictionaries, both print and digital, to determine or clarify the precise meaning of key words and phrases.	Determine or clarify the meaning of unknown and multiple-meaning words and phrases based on *grade 4 reading and content,* choosing flexibly from a range of strategies. a. Use context (e.g., definitions, examples, or restatements in text) as a clue to the meaning of a word or phrase. b. Use common, grade-appropriate Greek and Latin affixes and roots as clues to the meaning of a word (e.g., *telegraph, photograph, autograph*). c. Consult reference materials (e.g., dictionaries, glossaries, thesauruses), both print and digital, to find the pronunciation and determine or clarify the precise meaning of key words and phrases.	Determine or clarify the meaning of unknown and multiple-meaning words and phrases based on *grade 5 reading and content,* choosing flexibly from a range of strategies. a. Use context (e.g., cause/effect relationships or comparisons in text) as a clue to the meaning of a word or phrase. b. Use common, grade-appropriate Greek and Latin affixes and roots as clues to the meaning of a word (e.g., *photograph, photosynthesis*). c. Consult reference materials (e.g., dictionaries, glossaries, thesauruses), both print and digital, to find the pronunciation and determine or clarify the precise meaning of key words and phrases.

Continued

Table 1.1: K–5 Common Core Reading Standards Relevant to Teaching Children to Read, Understand, and Use Text Features across the Curriculum (*continued*)

Common Core	Grade K	Grade 1	Grade 2	Grade 3	Grade 4	Grade 5
Vocabulary Acquisition and Use	5. With guidance and support from adults, explore word relationships and nuances in word meanings. a. Sort common objects into categories (e.g., shapes, foods) to gain a sense of the concepts the categories represent. b. Demonstrate understanding of frequently occurring verbs and adjectives by relating them to their opposites (antonyms). c. Identify real-life connections between words and their use (e.g., note places at school that are *colorful*). d. Distinguish shades of meaning among verbs describing the same general action (e.g., *walk, march, strut, prance*) by acting out the meanings.	With guidance and support from adults, demonstrate understanding of word relationships and nuances in word meanings. a. Sort words into categories (e.g., colors, clothing) to gain a sense of the concepts the categories represent. b. Define words by category and by one or more key attributes (e.g., a *duck* is a bird that swims; a *tiger* is a large cat with stripes). c. Identify real-life connections between words and their use (e.g., note places at home that are *cozy*). d. Distinguish shades of meaning among verbs differing in manner (e.g., *look, peek, glance, stare, glare, scowl*) and adjectives differing in intensity (e.g., *large, gigantic*) by defining or choosing them or by acting out the meanings.	Demonstrate understanding of word relationships and nuances in word meanings. a. Identify real-life connections between words and their use (e.g., describe foods that are *spicy* or *juicy*). b. Distinguish shades of meaning among closely related verbs (e.g., *toss, throw, hurl*) and closely related adjectives (e.g., *thin, slender, skinny, scrawny*).	Demonstrate understanding of word relationships and nuances in word meanings. a. Distinguish the literal and nonliteral meanings of words and phrases in context (e.g., *take steps*). b. Identify real-life connections between words and their use (e.g., describe people who are *friendly* or *helpful*). c. Distinguish shades of meaning among related words that describe states of mind or degrees of certainty (e.g., *knew, believed, suspected, heard, wondered*).	Demonstrate understanding of figurative language, word relationships, and nuances in word meanings. a. Explain the meaning of simple similes and metaphors (e.g., *as pretty as a picture*) in context. b. Recognize and explain the meaning of common idioms, adages, and proverbs. c. Demonstrate understanding of words by relating them to their opposites (antonyms) and to words with similar but not identical meanings (synonyms).	Demonstrate understanding of figurative language, word relationships, and nuances in word meanings. a. Interpret figurative language, including similes and metaphors, in context. b. Recognize and explain the meaning of common idioms, adages, and proverbs. c. Use the relationship between particular words (e.g., synonyms, antonyms, homographs) to better understand each of the words.
Vocabulary Acquisition and Use	6. Use words and phrases acquired through conversations, reading and being read to, and responding to texts.	Use words and phrases acquired through conversations, reading and being read to, and responding to texts, including using frequently occurring conjunctions to signal simple relationships (e.g., *because*).	Use words and phrases acquired through conversations, reading and being read to, and responding to texts, including using adjectives and adverbs to describe (e.g., *When other kids are happy that makes me happy*).	Acquire and use accurately grade-appropriate conversational, general academic, and domain specific words and phrases, including those that signal spatial and temporal relationships (e.g., *After dinner that night we went looking for them*).	Acquire and use accurately grade-appropriate general academic and domain-specific words and phrases, including those that signal precise actions, emotions, or states of being (e.g., *quizzed, whined, stammered*) and that are basic to a particular topic (e.g., *wildlife, conservation*, and *endangered* when discussing animal preservation).	Acquire and use accurately grade-appropriate general academic and domain-specific words and phrases, including those that signal contrast, addition, and other logical relationships (e.g., *however, although, nevertheless, similarly, moreover, in addition*).

From www.corestandards.org/the-standards/english-language-arts-standards

122 | Reading the Whole Page

Appendix C
Knowledge of Text Features Assessment

Directions

1. The assessment area should be quiet and free from major distractions. Generally, a small table where you can sit beside the student is sufficient. You will need a computer if you plan to use the e-book on the CD. Have a copy of the *Knowledge of Text Features Assessment Score Sheet* available and the text(s) the student will be using to find and use text features. Remember the e-book can be printed as a paper book, too.

2. Preview the prompts for the *Knowledge of Text Features Assessment.* You may want to give only one section (print, graphic, or organizational) of the assessment at a time. For example, you may want to focus instruction on print features only, so you could just give this part as a pre-assessment. If you want to cover all three types of features, give the entire assessment. Write any anecdotal observations of the student's behaviors on the score sheet as you give the assessment.

3. Give the student a non-fiction text. Remember, you are assessing, so avoid guiding the student in the use of the text features beyond the suggested prompts. A script is offered to launch the assessment:

   Today I am going to ask you to identify some text features. A text feature is anything that is not in the main body of the text, like a title or a picture. I will also ask you to tell me what you know about each text feature. The text feature may be anywhere in the book, so you can look throughout the book to find the text feature. What I learn from this assessment will help me plan instruction to help you be a better reader. [Optional: You will not be graded on this assessment, but I do want you to try your best so I can know how to better help you grow as a reader.]

4. The columns labeled "Teacher Prompt" on the *Knowledge of Text Features Assessment Score Sheet* provide prompts for each task: identification, purpose, and application of a text feature (see image below). The student will first be asked to identify the text feature. If the student is

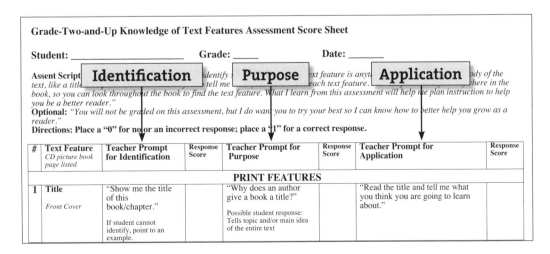

unable to locate the text feature, place a "0" in this column or highlight the box and then point to an example of the text feature. If the student looks to you for verification, try not to sway his or her selection. Remember this is an assessment and not instruction. Next, follow the prompts for knowing the purpose and application of this feature to aid comprehension. You may point to a feature once the child has indicated he can't find it, but do not tell him the purpose of the text feature. If the student is a non-reader, you will have to read the text feature to him. If the student can identify the text feature correctly, place a "1" in the column, ask the prompt related to the purpose (you are given a possible student response as a guide), and then have him read the text feature to demonstrate application.

5. The student receives a point for a correct response related to each task. Possible answers for the purpose of each text feature are given, but application responses will vary based on the text feature and content. The student does not need to provide exact wording, but the gist of his response should match the definition in order to be recorded as correct. Record any incorrect responses in the assessment observations column for later analysis.

6. After giving the assessment, reflect on the student's performance, and choose one or both scoring options, depending on your needs: individual student scores and/or a class profile.

7. Total the number of correct responses in each column for each section, and record the totals in the table located at the bottom of the score sheet. You will have a total for each section: identification, purpose, and application.

8. Complete the *Knowledge of Text Features Class Profile*. Completing this profile will allow you to capture your entire class's knowledge of text features on one sheet of paper. Student names should be listed vertically, and performance is noted for each feature horizontally. The scoring code indicates that the student identified the text feature (I), understood the purpose (P), and/or applied the text feature to reading/learning (A). At the bottom of each column, total the number of students who identify, know the purpose of, and apply each feature. Highlight a cell if the student needs more support with any or all of the levels of text feature knowledge (identifying, knowing the purpose, and/or applying). If a cell is left blank, that would indicate that the student does not have any knowledge of this text feature and needs explicit instruction on this feature. Note: It is not necessary to re-administer the entire *Knowledge of Text Features Assessment* to every student. For some students, it is sufficient to re-administer only the sections on which they had difficulty and/or those that you taught.

9. Analyze the student's correct and incorrect responses (along with your observations of his behavior) about text features to determine strengths and areas in need of instruction. Analyze the student's response by task (identification, purpose, and application) and category (print, graphic, and organizational) for each text feature. Because the assessment is designed developmentally, the student may or may not progress beyond identifying the text feature. If you find that a student had difficulty with the identification of a text feature, then instruction begins there. If the student could identify the text feature but was unable to state its purpose, then instruction begins there. Some students may be able to apply the text feature when reading but not be metacognitive regarding its purpose. Looking at the section categories (print, graphic, and organizational) and then the tasks (identify, determine purpose, and apply while reading) will help you to differentiate your instruction.

*For each assessment, there is a score sheet and class profile (kindergarten/first grade and grades two and up), all of which are also available on the CD.

K-1 Knowledge of Text Features Assessment Score Sheet

Student _____   Grade _____   Date _____

Assent Script: *"Today I am going to ask you to identify some text features. A text feature is anything that is not in the main body of the text, like a title or a picture. I will also ask you to tell me what you know about each text feature. The text feature may be anywhere in the book, so you can look throughout the book to find the text feature. What I learn from this assessment will help me plan instruction to help you be a better reader."*

Optional: *"You will not be graded on this assessment but I do want you to try your best so I can know how to better help you grow as a reader."*

Directions: Place a "0" for no or incorrect response; place a "1" for a correct response.

#	Text Feature CD picture book page listed	Teacher Prompt for Identification	Response Score	Teacher Prompt for Purpose	Response Score	Teacher Prompt for Application	Response Score
			PRINT FEATURES				
1	**Title** *Front Cover*	"Show me the title of this book/ chapter." If student cannot identify, point to an example.		"Why does an author give a book a title?" Possible student response: Tells topic and/or main idea of the entire text		"Read the title and tell me what you think you are going to learn about."	
2	**Heading/ Subheading** *Heading: p. 2, 3, 6, 7, 10 Subheading: p. 4, 8, 9*	"Show me a heading/ subheading in this book." If student cannot identify, point to an example.		"Why does an author give a heading/ subheading?" Possible student response: Tells the main idea of a section of text		"Read the heading/subheading and tell me what you think you are going to learn about."	
3	**Bold Print** *p. 3, 7, 8*	"Show me bold print." If student cannot identify, point to an example.		"Why does an author use bold print?" Possible student response: Shows important vocabulary in the text		"Read the bold print and tell me what you expect to learn about."	
4	**Caption** *p. 2, 3, 7–11*	"Show me a caption." If student cannot identify, point to an example.		"Why does an author use a caption?" Possible student response: Explains the picture it is nearest to		"Read the caption. What did you learn about the graphic feature (picture, photo, drawing) from the caption?"	

Continued

#	Text Feature *CD picture book page listed*	Teacher Prompt for Identification	Response Score	Teacher Prompt for Purpose	Response Score	Teacher Prompt for Application	Response Score
5	**Pronunciation Guide** *p. 3,7,10*	"Show me a pronunciation guide." If student cannot identify, point to an example.		"Why does an author use a pronunciation guide?" Possible student response: Shows how to pronounce or say a new or unusual word		"Use the pronunciation guide to pronounce the word."	
				GRAPHIC FEATURES			
6	**Photograph with or without caption** *p. 2, 3, 7–11*	"Show me a photograph." If student cannot identify, point to an example.		"Why does an author put a photograph in a book?" Possible student response: Helps you see real events, steps, or objects described in the text		"Look at the photograph and explain why you think this is in the text/chapter/book."	
7	**Drawing with or without caption** *p. 9*	"Show me a drawing." If student cannot identify, point to an example.		"Why does an author put a drawing in a book?" Possible student response: Helps you see something from the text		"Look at the drawing and explain why you think this is in the text/chapter/book."	
8	**Inset** *p. 9*	"Show me an inset." If student cannot identify, point to an example.		"Why does an author put an inset in a book?" Possible student response: Helps you see something in the text in large and small scale		"Look at the inset and explain why you think this is in the text/chapter/book."	
9	**Diagram** *p. 7, 9–10*	"Show me a diagram." If student cannot identify, point to an example.		"Why does an author put a diagram in a book?" Possible student response: Explains steps in a process or how something is made		"Read the diagram. What did you learn?"	
10	Labeled Diagram *p. 7*	"Show me a labeled diagram." If student cannot identify, point to an example.		"Why does an author put a labeled diagram in a book?" Possible student response: Shows the different parts of something in the text		"Read the labeled diagram. What did you learn?"	

Continued

#	Text Feature CD picture book page listed	Teacher Prompt for Identification	Response Score	Teacher Prompt for Purpose	Response Score	Teacher Prompt for Application	Response Score
11	**Map** *p. 4–5*	"Show me a map." If student cannot identify, point to an example.		"Why does an author put a map in a book?" Possible student response: Shows the location or impact of something in the text		"Read the map. What did you learn?"	
12	**Graph** *p. 6*	"Show me a graph." If student cannot identify, point to an example.		"Why does an author put a graph in a book?" Possible student response: Shows data and/or displays information important to the text		"Read the graph. What did you learn?"	
13	**Timeline** *p. 6*	"Show me a timeline." If student cannot identify, point to an example.		"Why does an author put a timeline in a book? Possible student response: Allows you to see when events in the text occurred		"Read the timeline. What did you learn?"	
	ORGANIZATIONAL FEATURES						
14	**Table of Contents** *p. 1*	"Show me a table of contents." If student cannot identify, point to an example.		"Why does an author have a table of contents?" Possible student response: Helps you quickly find the topic you are seeking		Point to a section of the TOC: "Read this and tell me what topics will be in this book/text." "Where will I find information on _____?" (Fill in the blank with a topic that would be found in this book.)	
15	**Index** *p. 13*	"Show me an index." If student cannot identify, point to an example.		"Why does an author have an index? Possible student response: Helps you quickly find the specific information they are seeking is located		Look at the index and identify a topic: "On what page(s) can you find the topic?"	
16	**Glossary** *p. 12*	"Show me a glossary." If student cannot identify, point to an example.		"Why does an author have a glossary?" Possible student response: Gives you the definition of new or text-critical words		Look at the glossary and identify a word: "What is the definition of this word?"	

Key: 0 = no response or wrong response; 1 = correct response

Continued

Total and transfer scores to the table below:

Text Feature Category	Identification	Purpose	Application	Specific Observations
Print Features	___/5	___/5	___/5	
Graphic Features	___/8	___/8	___/8	
Organizational Features	___/3	___/3	___/3	

Note: Use the information from this assessment to plot on the *K-1 Knowledge of Text Features Assessment Class Profile* whether a student can identify, knows the purpose, and/or applies each text feature.

K-1 Knowledge of Text Features Assessment Class Profile

Teacher's Name _____   Grade _____   Date _____

Students' Names	Print Features					Graphic Features								Organizational Features		
	Title	Heading/ Subheading	Bold Print	Caption	Pron. Guide	Photo	Drawing	Inset	Diagram	Labeled Diagram	Map	Graph	Timeline	TOC	Index	Glossary
# who identify:																
# who know purpose:																
# who apply:																

Key: I = Identifies; P = Knows Purpose; A = Applies

Grade-Two-and-Up Knowledge of Text Features Assessment Score Sheet

Student _____ Grade _____ Date _____

Assent Script: *"Today I am going to ask you to identify some text features. A text feature is anything that is not in the main body of the text, like a title or a picture. I will also ask you to tell me what you know about each text feature. The text feature may be anywhere in the book, so you can look throughout the book to find the text feature. What I learn from this assessment will help me plan instruction to help you be a better reader."*

Optional: *"You will not be graded on this assessment but I do want you to try your best so I can know how to better help you grow as a reader."*

Directions: Place a "0" for no or incorrect response; place a "1" for a correct response.

#	Text Feature CD picture book page listed	Teacher Prompt for Identification	Response Score	Teacher Prompt for Purpose	Response Score	Teacher Prompt for Application	Response Score
				PRINT FEATURES			
1	**Title** *Front Cover*	"Show me the title of this book/chapter." If student cannot identify, point to an example.		"Why does an author give a book a title?" Possible student response: Tells topic and/or main idea of the entire text		"Read the title and tell me what you think you are going to learn about."	
2	**Heading/ Subheading** *Heading: p. 2, 3, 6, 7, 10 Subheading: p. 4, 8, 9*	"Show me a heading/subheading in this book." If student cannot identify, point to an example.		"Why does an author give a heading/ subheading?" Possible student response: Tells the main idea of a section of text		"Read the heading/subheading and tell me what you think you are going to learn about."	
3	**Bold Print** *p. 3, 7, 8*	"Show me bold print." If student cannot identify, point to an example.		"Why does an author use bold print?" Possible student response: Shows important vocabulary in the text		"Read the bold print and tell me what you expect to learn about."	
4	**Italics** *p. 9*	"Show me italics." If student cannot identify, point to an example.		"Why does an author use italics?" Possible student response: Shows important vocabulary or emphasize a word when reading		"Read the italicized print and tell me what you expect to learn about."	

Continued

#	Text Feature *CD picture book page listed*	Teacher Prompt for Identification	Response Score	Teacher Prompt for Purpose	Response Score	Teacher Prompt for Application	Response Score
5	**Caption** *p. 2, 3, 7–11*	"Show me a caption." If student cannot identify, point to an example.		"Why does an author use a caption?" Possible student response: Explains the picture it is nearest to		"Read the caption. What did you learn about the graphic feature (picture, photo, drawing) from the caption?"	
6	**Pronunciation Guide** *p. 3, 7, 10*	"Show me a pronunciation guide." If student cannot identify, point to an example.		"Why does an author use a pronunciation guide?" Possible student response: Shows how to pronounce or say a new or unusual word		"Use the pronunciation guide to pronounce the word."	
7	**Bullets** *p. 7*	"Show me bullets." If student cannot identify, point to an example.		"Why does an author use bullets?" Possible student response: Emphasizes and condenses big ideas in a text		"Read the bullets and tell me what was important in this section of text."	
8	**Sidebar** *p. 11*	"Show me a sidebar." If student cannot identify, point to an example.		"Why does an author use a sidebar?" Possible student response: Provides additional details, facts, or information related to the text		"Read the sidebar. What did you learn?"	
				GRAPHIC FEATURES			
9	**Photograph with or without caption** *p. 2, 3, 7–11*	"Show me a photograph." If student cannot identify, point to an example.		"Why does an author put a photograph in a book?" Possible student response: Helps you see real events, steps, or objects described in the text		"Look at the photograph and explain why you think this is in the text/chapter/book."	
10	**Drawing with or without caption** *p. 9*	"Show me a drawing." If student cannot identify, point to an example.		"Why does an author put a drawing in a book?" Possible student response: Helps you see something from the text		"Look at the drawing and explain why you think this is in the text/chapter/book."	

Continued

#	Text Feature *CD picture book page listed*	Teacher Prompt for Identification	Response Score	Teacher Prompt for Purpose	Response Score	Teacher Prompt for Application	Response Score
11	**Inset** *p. 9*	"Show me an inset." If student cannot identify, point to an example.		"Why does an author put an inset in a book?" Possible student response: Helps you see something in the text in large and small scale		"Look at the inset and explain why you think this is in the text/chapter/book."	
12	**Cross-section/ Cutaway** *p. 9*	"Show me a cross-section or cutaway." If student cannot identify, point to an example.		"Why does an author use a cross-section/ cutaway in a book?" Possible student response: Helps you see all the layers or the interior and exterior of a person, place, or thing in the text		"Look at the cross-section/ cutaway and explain why you think this is in the text/chapter/ book."	
13	**Diagram** *p. 7, 9–10*	"Show me a diagram." If student cannot identify, point to an example.		"Why does an author put a diagram in a book?" Possible student response: Explains steps in a process or how something is made		"Read the diagram. What did you learn?"	
14	**Labeled Diagram** *p. 7*	"Show me a labeled diagram." If student cannot identify, point to an example.		"Why does an author put a labeled diagram in a book?" Possible student response: Shows the different parts of something in the text		"Read the labeled diagram. What did you learn?"	
15	**Map** *p. 4–5*	"Show me a map." If student cannot identify, point to an example.		"Why does an author put a map in a book?" Possible student response: Shows the location or impact of something in the text		"Read the map. What did you learn?"	
16	**Graph** *p. 6*	"Show me a graph." If student cannot identify, point to an example.		"Why does an author put a graph in a book?" Possible student response: Shows data and/or displays information important to the text		"Read the graph. What did you learn?"	

Continued

#	Text Feature CD picture book page listed	Teacher Prompt for Identification	Response Score	Teacher Prompt for Purpose	Response Score	Teacher Prompt for Application	Response Score
17	**Timeline** p. 6	"Show me a timeline." If student cannot identify, point to an example.		"What does an author put a timeline in a book?" Possible student response: Allows you to see when events in the text occurred		"Read the timeline. What did you learn?"	
18	**Chart/Table** p. 10	"Show me a chart/table." If student cannot identify, point to an example.		"Why does an author put a chart/table in a book?" Possible student response: Organizes and displays data in the text easily		"Read the chart/table. What did you learn?"	
	ORGANIZATIONAL FEATURES						
19	**Table of Contents** p. 1	"Show me a table of contents." If student cannot identify, point to an example.		"Why does an author have a table of contents?" Possible student response: Helps you quickly find the topic you are seeking		Point to a section of the TOC: "Read this and tell me what topics will be in this book/text." "Where will I find information on _____?" (Fill in the blank with a topic that would be found in this book.)	
20	**Index** p. 13	"Show me an index." If student cannot identify, point to an example.		"Why does an author have an index?" Possible student response: Helps you quickly find the specific information they are seeking is located		Look at the index and identify a topic: "On what page(s) can you find the topic?"	
21	**Glossary** p. 12	"Show me a glossary." If student cannot identify, point to an example.		"Why does an author have a glossary?" Possible student response: Gives you the definition of new or text-critical words		Look at the glossary and identify a word: "What is the definition of this word?"	

Continued

Key: 0 = no response or wrong response; 1 = correct response

Total and transfer scores to the table below:

Text Feature Category	Identification	Purpose	Application	Specific Observations
Print Features	___/8	___/8	___/8	
Graphic Features	___/10	___/10	___/10	
Organizational Features	___/3	___/3	___/3	

Note: Use the information from this assessment to plot on the *K-1 Knowledge of Text Features Assessment Class Profile* whether a student can identify, knows the purpose, and/or applies each text feature.

Grade-Two-and-Up Knowledge of Text Features Assessment Class Profile

Teacher's Name _____   Grade _____   Date _____

Students' Names	Print Features								Graphic Features											Organizational Features		
	Title	Heading/ Subheading	Bold Print	Italics	Caption	Pron. Guide	Bullets	Sidebar	Photo	Drawing	Inset	Cross-section/ Cutaway	Diagram	Labeled Diagram	Map	Graph	Chart/Table	Timeline	TOC	Index	Glossary
# who identify:																						
# who know purpose:																						
# who apply:																						

Key: I = Identifies; P = Knows Purpose; A = Applies

Appendix D
Suggested Resources for Teaching Text Features

Series	Publisher	Grade	Text Features Used	Notes
Explorations	Okapi Educational Publishers Publishing	K-6	Primary texts include table of contents, headings, diagrams, pictures, captions, index, and glossary; intermediate texts include the same plus maps, drawings, sidebars, labeled diagrams, bullets, and bold print	Books available for the interactive whiteboard
iOpeners	Pearson	K-6	Includes all features listed on our text feature matrix: table of contents, headings, diagrams, pictures, captions, index, glossary, maps, drawings, sidebars, labeled diagrams, bullets, cutaways/cross-sections, charts, graphs, timelines, insets, italics, and bold print	Broad range of text features within each book at all levels
Multi-level Non-fiction Books	Lakeshore Learning Materials	1-6	Includes table of contents, headings, diagrams, pictures, captions, index, glossary, maps, drawings, sidebars, labeled diagrams, bullets, cutaways/cross-sections, charts, graphs, timelines, insets, italics, and bold print	Broad range of text features within each book at all levels; topics are addressed at three different levels within each set
My Science Library	Rourke Publishing, LLC	K-3	Includes titles, headings, table of contents, index, glossary (some picture glossaries), and labeled diagrams	Each title contains good examples of a limited number of text features
Weekly Reader	Weekly Reader	Pre-K-6	Includes titles, headings, bold print, italics, pronunciation guides, sidebars, diagrams, labeled diagrams, pictures, captions, timelines, maps, charts, graphs, and bullets	Online digital editions with links for use on interactive whiteboard or PC; primary editions contain fewer text features
Time for Kids	Time, Inc.	K-6	Includes titles, headings, bold print, italics, pronunciation guides, sidebars, diagrams, labeled diagrams, pictures, captions, timelines, maps, charts, graphs, bullets, and glossary box	Online digital editions with links for use on interactive whiteboard or PC; primary editions contain fewer text features
Scholastic News	Scholastic, Inc.	K-6	Includes titles, headings, bold print, pronunciation guides, sidebars, pictures, captions, timelines, maps, charts, graphs, bullets, and glossary box	Online digital editions with links for use on interactive whiteboard or PC; primary editions contain fewer text features

Appendix E
Thinksheets

Thinksheets for
CHAPTER 2

Thinksheet 2.1: Give Your Book a Title

Name: _____

Directions: Find the headings that fit with the title below. Write the chapter titles in the box with the title.

Book Title: <u>From Blossom to Fruit</u>
Chapter Titles:

Now write the rest of the chapter titles below. Make up and write a title for a book that these chapter headings might be in.

Chapter Titles:

My Made-up Book Title:

Thinksheet 2.2: Chapter Title Sort Cards

From Blossom to Fruit

Blossoms	**Fruit**
Seeds	**Apples**
Boats	**Bicycles**
Cars	**Wagons**

Picking Apples

Equipment
Picking Apples
Oranges
Shipping Oranges
Shipping Apples
Picking Oranges
Making Apple Juice
Making Orange Juice

Unusual Animals: Parrot

The Unusual Parrots
Cool Cacti
How Parrots Look
How Plants Look
Where Parrots Live
What Plants Need
Meat-eating Plants
Purple Plants
Kinds of Parrots
Baby Parrots

Your Teeth

Kinds of Teeth
Parts of Eyes
Parts of Teeth
Seeing
Baby Teeth
Your Eyes
Permanent Teeth
Colors of Eyes

FROM TADPOLE TO FROG

A FROG EGG
A BUTTERFLY EGG
A TADPOLE GROWS
A CHRYSALIS
A FULL-GROWN FROG

Land Mammals

Western Gray Squirrels
What Western Gray Squirrels Eat
Baby Gray Squirrel

Gray Whales

Gray Whales
What Whales Look Like
What Whales Eat
Where Whales Live
Living in the Forest
Baby Gray Whales
Saving Gray Whales

Thinksheet 2.3: Create a Cover

Name: _____

Directions

1. Read your chapter title cards and think about what type of book these chapters would be in.
2. Decide on a title for your book and write it on the book cover, next to the word *Title*.
3. Decide in which order the chapter titles might be in this book. Write the chapter titles in this order in the table of contents.
4. Draw a picture on your cover.

Table of Contents

Chapter 1: _____

Chapter 2: _____

Chapter 3: _____

Chapter 4: _____

Chapter 5: _____

Glossary

Index

Title: _____

Thinksheet 2.4: Help! Animals Need to Be Rescued Article

Help! Animals Need to Be Rescued
By Nicki Clausen-Grace

Millions of Lonely Pets

Every year, millions of pets are locked in kennels without anyone to love them because they have been abandoned by their owners. These cats and dogs usually haven't done anything wrong; their owners just don't want them any more. Sometimes the owners have died or lost a job, so they can't afford to care for their pets.

Where Are These Lonely Pets?

The luckiest of these pets are kept in shelters that help look for new owners. The less lucky animals get picked up by the county where they are put to sleep if no one claims them. All of these places feed the animals while they are in their care. They just don't have the time or money to play with them.

What You Can Do to Help

One way you can help is by never buying a puppy from a store. Instead, visit a shelter and adopt a lonely pet. Another way you can help is by making sure you can care for your pet for his whole life. Many shelters accept donations of money or food. Some even allow people to volunteer to clean crates, feed the animals, or take the dogs for walks. Everyone should do what he or she can to take care of these lonely pets.

Thinksheet 2.5: **Bold** and *Italic* Word Detective

Name: _____

Name of Text: _____

Word	Page # found	Is it **bold** or *italic?*	Why I think the author used **bold** or *italicized* print…

Thinksheet 2.6: Caption Match Sorting Cards

Graphic Feature Cards	Caption Cards
	Dogs eat kibble and dog bones.
	This shows the inside of a dog's ear.
	Dogs make good pets.
	Dogs need to be walked on a leash every day.

Thinksheet 2.7: Where Does It Fit?

Directions: Cut out each picture and caption. Read and decide which book each picture/caption would be in. Glue the picture and caption under the correct title on the T-chart your teacher gave you (next page).

Squirrels like to eat acorns. They eat some now and save some for later.

Boys and girls wear t-shirts. They are comfortable and go with many different outfits.

Jeans are comfortable and warm to wear. Lots of kids wear jeans.

Owls mostly come out at night. They eat smaller animals.

Most kids wear tennis shoes at least sometimes.

Bears eat almost anything in the forest.

Deer eat plants. Some people eat deer.

Animals of the Forest	**Our Clothes**

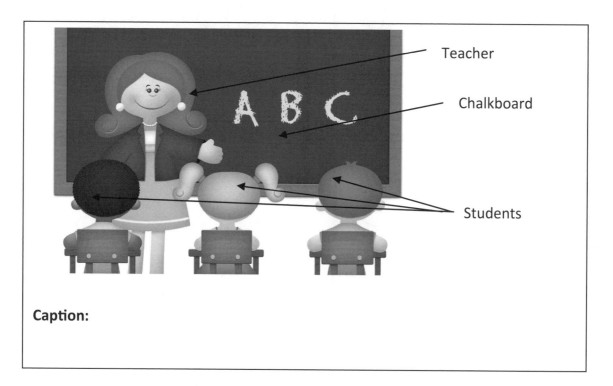

Teacher

Chalkboard

Students

Caption:

School

School is a good place to learn. Kids go to school to learn to read, write, and solve math problems. They learn map skills and science, too. Some children walk and some children ride, but every child should go to school.

Caption:

Caption:

Thinksheet 2.9: Text Bullets

Electricity

Most people use electricity every day. Electricity makes things run. It makes lights light up. It makes computers turn on. It makes televisions play. It powers the heat in our homes. It would be hard to live without electricity.

Electricity powers:

- Lights
- Computers
- Televisions
- Heaters

Cars

People use cars to drive places. Cars can be really big, like a **limousine**. Cars can be really small like a Smart Car. Most cars use gas, and some cars use electricity. Almost all cars have:

- Four wheels
- Windows
- A steering wheel
- Headlights

The Model T
Henry Ford began selling Model T Fords in 1908. Not many people had cars in 1908, but a lot that did have cars owned Model Ts.

window
headlight
wheel

Bicycles

Bicycles can help people go places, too. They don't use gas or electricity; they use manpower (or kidpower, when kids ride them!). Bicycles have:

- Two wheels
- Handlebars
- Brakes

There are many different types of bicycles, including road bikes, mountain bikes, and beach bikes.

Thinksheet 2.10: Reading Bullets

Name: _____

Directions: Read each set of bullets. Underneath, write what you learned from reading the bullets and come up with a possible title for a book you might find these bullets in.

1) Horses need:
- Water
- Food
- Shoes
- Exercise

What I learned from reading the bullets: _____

_____

These bullets might be in a book with this title: _____

_____

2) Girls wear:
- Shirts
- Shorts
- Pants
- Skirts
- Dresses

What I learned from reading the bullets: _____

_____

These bullets might be in a book with this title: _____

_____

3) If you want to play baseball you must have:
- A ball
- A bat
- Bases
- Gloves
- Other players

What I learned from reading the bullets: _____

_____

These bullets might be in a book with this title: _____

_____

Thinksheet 2.11: All about Me in Bullets   Name: _____

Directions: Complete the sentences and fill in the bullets to tell your classmates about yourself.

Tell who you are. _____

_____

_____

Tell where you live or what you like to do. _____

_____

I have:

- _____ (color of eyes)

- _____ (color of hair)

- _____ (one other thing)

Draw a picture of yourself here:

Caption: _____

Thinksheet 2.12: Using Bullets to Summarize   Name: _____

Directions: Read each paragraph, and choose one part to summarize using bullets. Remember that the bullets all need to be about the same topic.

1) Cooking
Cooking is a great way to have fun and make treats for your family and friends. You can make cookies. You can make a cake. You can even make hamburgers. The one thing you cannot make is the tools you need for cooking. You need bowls. You need spoons. You need pans. You need measuring cups. If you have all the tools and ingredients, you can cook food that tastes great.

Write the stem and bullets here: _____

- _____
- _____
- _____
- _____

2) Football
Many children want to play football when they grow up. Not many people get to have this job, though. If you want to be a professional football player, you need to be big. You need to be strong. You need to have talent. You also need to be hardworking and lucky. It is probably a good idea to have another job in mind in case you don't end up playing football.

Write the stem and bullets here: _____

- _____
- _____
- _____
- _____

3) Matter
Everything that takes up space and has mass is called **matter**. Candy is matter. Juice is matter. Even air is matter. There are three different forms of matter. The first is **solid**. The second is **liquid**. The last is **gas.** Even you are made of matter.

Write the stem and bullets here: _____

- _____
- _____
- _____
- _____

Thinksheet 2.13: Which Sidebar Fits?

Directions: Draw a line to match each sidebar with the main body of text it might go with. Remember, a sidebar is related to the main body of text but goes into more detail about one part.

Main Body of Text	Sidebar
What Is Weather? Weather happens every day. It is the condition of the sky above and the outside air all around us. Weather can change by the hour or by the day. It can also stay the same for many days or weeks.	Lightning is a flash of electricity produced by a thunderstorm.
	A tornado is also called a twister. It can smash buildings to pieces.
Stormy Weather **Thunder** and **lightning** can happen during stormy weather. Rain, hail, or snow may fall from the sky.	Look at these snowflakes; no two are alike.
Snowflakes form in clouds when water droplets freeze. A **blizzard** is a storm with lots of snow.	Some locations have lots of sunny, warm weather.
A **tornado** is a violent windstorm. It looks like a dark cloud shaped like a funnel.	Blue skies can quickly turn gray.

(Some excerpts from Storad C. (2012). *What's the Weather Like Today?* Vero Beach, FL: Rourke Publishing LLC)

Thinksheets for
CHAPTER 3

Thinksheet 3.1: Which Picture?

Directions: Match the story description to the appropriate picture by drawing a line from the picture to the story description. Then draw a picture to go with the story description you are given in part B.

A. Matching

Story Descriptions

a. This story is going to be about my uncle who ran in his first marathon.

1.

b. This story is going to be about my new puppy, Maggie.

2.

c. This story is going to be about my grandmother's flower garden.

3.

B. Think about what you would draw to go along with a story about a girl winning the volleyball championships. Then, create a picture on the back of this paper to go with this story.

Thinksheet 3.2: Set in What?

Directions: Match the insets below with the larger photos they would be a part of. Cut each picture out and glue it on paper to make a photo with an inset. Write a short caption for each inset.

Larger Pictures	Insets

Name: _____

Thinksheet 3.3: Inset Hunt

Book or chapter title/page number	What does the large picture show?	What does the small picture show?

Thinksheet 3.4: Cross-section Hunt

Name: _____

Title of cross-section	Page number	Book or text title

Thinksheet 3.5: Explain It! Creating a Diagram

Name:_____

1. What are you explaining with your diagram?

    _____

2. What are some possible titles for your diagram?

    a. _____

    b. _____

    c. _____

3. Think about what you are explaining. What happens first? Use the stems below to help you draft the steps.

    Step 1: First, _____

    _____

    Step 2: Next, _____

    _____

    Step 3: Then, _____

    _____

    Step 4: Next, _____

    _____

    Step 5: Last, _____

    _____

4. Re-read your steps. Do you need to add any more details and/or steps? Fix and add any steps above.

5. For each step, list a possible picture that would be helpful in explaining the step. Also, include any labels that you think would be helpful.

Picture	What step or steps might help explain this picture?	What labels might go with this picture?

Thinksheet 3.6: Diagram Rubric

Criteria	0	1	2
Title	No title	Has a title, but title does not match the diagram's purpose	Title matches diagram's purpose
Labels	No labels	Labels included but do not identify important parts	Labels included and identify important parts of the diagram
Photograph, picture, or drawing	No photo, picture, or drawing	There are photos, pictures, or drawings, but not all are relevant to diagram's purpose	There are photos, pictures, or drawings relevant to diagram's purpose
Arrows, numbers, and/or lines	No arrows, numbers, and/or lines	Arrows, numbers, or lines are used to indicate at least two steps or the order in which to read the diagram	Arrows, numbers, and/or lines are used to indicate at least three steps or the order to read the diagram
Correctness	Many mistakes	Few mistakes (three to five)	Few or no mistakes (zero to two)
Neatness	Diagram is messy	Diagram could be neater	Diagram is neat

Thinksheet 3.7: Parts of a Map: What Am I?

Name: _____

Directions: Use the following terms to fill in each part of the map: key or legend, scale, pointer or compass rose, and title.

1. _____

2. _____

Roads and Stop Signs in My Town

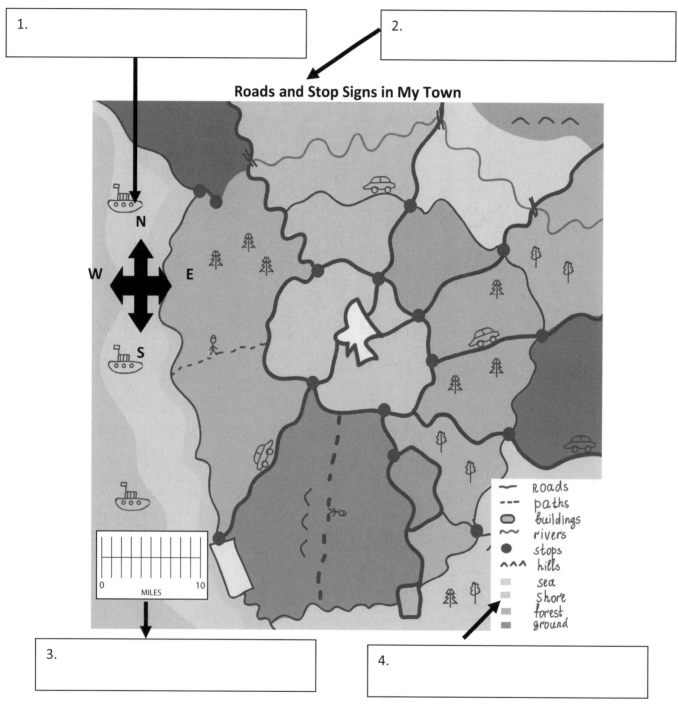

3. _____

4. _____

Bonus

1. What are the lines that run east to west called?

2. What are the lines that run north to south called?

Thinksheet 3.8: Creating a Map   Name: _____

1. My map will be of _____.

2. A good title for my map would be:

   _____.

3. List some of the items/places you will have on your map.

   _____

   _____

4. My legend/key will include the following symbols to represent an item/place (from number 3):

Symbol   **Item/Place**

☐	=	
☐	=	
☐	=	
☐	=	

5. Draw a draft of your compass rose here:

6. Scale: If you are going to use a scale, what measuring unit will you use? _____ Metric _____ Standard

Thinksheet 3.9: Map Rubric

Criteria	0	1	2
Title	No title	Has a title, but it does not match the map	Title matches map
Scale	No scale	Has a scale but not always used	Scale present and always used
Legend/Key	No legend/key	Legend/key with one or two symbols	Legend/key with two or more symbols
Compass Rose	No compass rose	Compass rose has one to two directions on it	Compass rose has more than two directions on it
Correctness	Many mistakes	Few mistakes (three to five)	Few or no mistakes (zero to two)
Neatness	Map is messy	Map could be neater	Map is neat

© 2012 Michelle Kelley & Nicki Clausen-Grace, *Reading the Whole Page*

Appendix E | Thinksheets for Chapter 3

Three Little Pigs Timeline

The pigs leave home.

- 1st pig builds straw house
- 2nd pig builds stick house
- 3rd pig builds brick house

The wolf goes down the chimney into a pot of boiling water.

- Wolf gets greedy, asks pig for all these things
- 3rd pig tricks wolf

The Big Bad Wolf comes looking for food.

- Wolf blows down straw house
- Wolf blows down stick house
- Wolf tries to blow down brick house and can't

The History of Candy in America

Directions: Draw a line from the pictures of the candy to where they belong on the timeline.

| 1900 |

| 1880 |

| 1800 |

| 1880 | Candy corn was invented.

| 1908 | The lollipop was invented.

| 1800 | Penny candy (boiled sugar candy) was made in Colonial America.

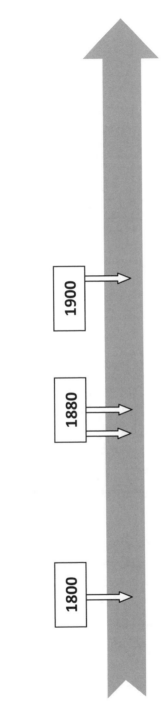

| 1875 | Milk chocolate was invented.

Thinksheet 3.12: Timeline Organizer

Use this table to record information for your timeline.

Number/order of events	Date/year	Event	Picture or symbol

Thinksheet 3.13: Timeline Rubric

Criteria	0	1	2
Title	No title	Title present but does not give the main idea of the timeline	Title matches timeline's purpose
Labels/captions	No labels/captions	Labels/captions included but do not explain events/ideas on timeline	Labels/captions included and explain events/ideas on timeline
Photograph, picture, and/or drawing	No photo, picture, and/or drawing	Photos, pictures, and/or drawings but not all are relevant to timeline	There are photos, pictures, and/or drawings relevant to timeline
Arrow, numbers, and/or line	No arrow, numbers, and/or line	Arrow, numbers, and/or line sometimes used to indicate the order of the events on the timeline	Arrow, numbers, and/or line used to indicate the order of the events on the timeline
Dates in order	Dates missing or some dates missing; dates may or may not be in order	Includes dates but may or may not be in order	Dates included and in order
Neatness	Timeline is messy	Timeline could be neater	Timeline is neat

Thinksheet 3.14: What Am I? The Anatomy of a Graph

Name: _____

Directions: Write the parts of the graph in bold print inside the correct empty box.

1. **Title** of the graph. This tells the reader what the graph is about.
2. **Horizontal axis:** The groups (subject) on the graph that go across the bottom of the graph.
3. **Vertical axis:** The number (or frequency) of the groups (subject) on the graph that go on the side of the graph.
4. **Scale:** The scale is the amount or frequency on the side axis.

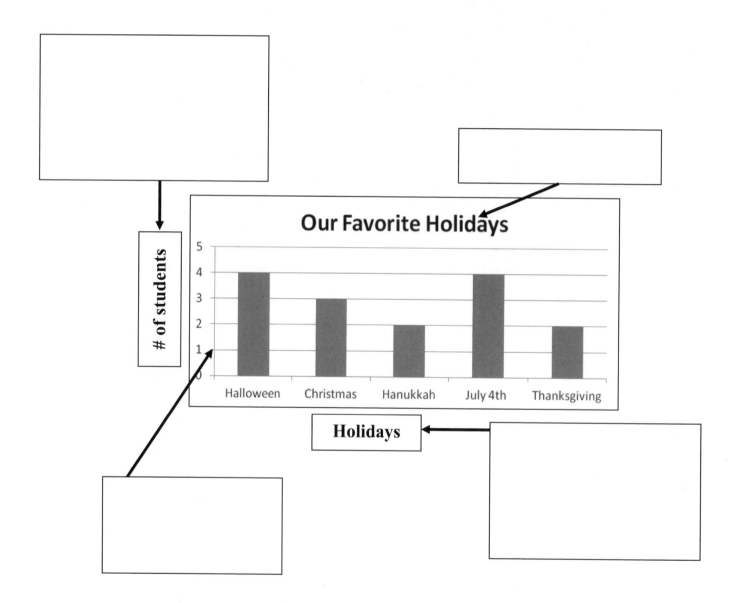

Name: _____

Directions: Use the following graph to answer the questions below.

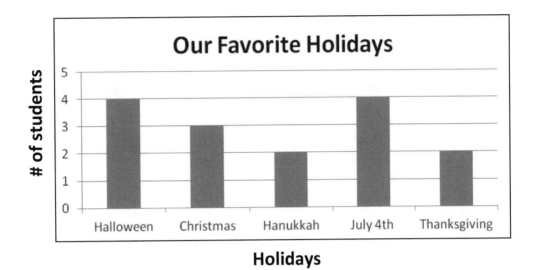

1. What is this graph about?

   _____

2. What holiday do three students say is their favorite?

   _____

3. What two holidays have the most votes?

   _____

4. How many students like Thanksgiving the best? _____

5. How many students voted for a favorite holiday? _____

Thinksheet 3.16: Creating a Favorites Graph

Name: _____

Directions: Decide what data you want to collect. Some examples include: favorite color, ice cream, sport, book, or music.

1. Which favorite will you collect data on? _____
   (your subject)

2. Brainstorm possible favorites for your subject that could be voted on by your class.

   _____   _____

   _____   _____

   _____   _____

   _____   _____

3. From your list in number 2 above, choose five favorites to ask your classmates to vote on. Put a star (*) next to them or highlight them (in number 2). Write them in the tally chart below under the column labeled "Favorite." Ask classmates to place a tally mark to show what their favorite is (see holiday example below).

Favorite (your subject)	Tallies (votes by students)
1.	
2.	
3.	
4.	
5.	

Example

Favorite Holiday	Tallies (votes by students)
1. Halloween	1111
2. Christmas	111
3. Hanukkah	11
4. July 4th	1111
5. Thanksgiving	11

4. Create a bar graph using your tally chart data (see number 3). Include a title and labels for axes (horizontal X and vertical Y).

Example

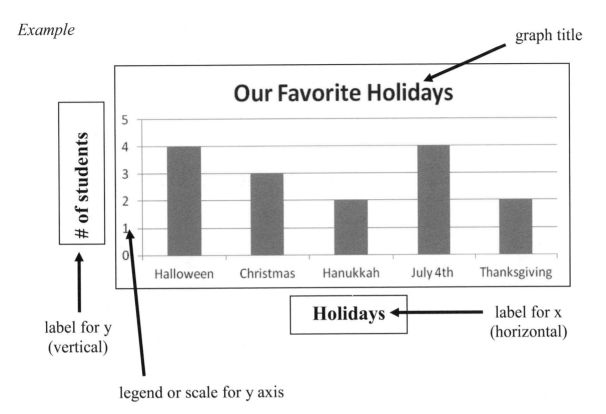

graph title

# of students

label for y (vertical)

legend or scale for y axis

Holidays

label for x (horizontal)

Thinksheet 3.17: What's Your Favorite _____?

Name: _____

Directions: Decide what data you want to collect. Some examples include: favorite color, ice cream, sport, book, or music.

1. Which favorite will you collect data on? _____
   (your subject)

2. Brainstorm possible favorites for your subject that could be voted on by your class.

   _____   _____

   _____   _____

   _____   _____

   _____

3. From your list in number 2 above, choose five favorites to ask your classmates to vote on. Put a star (*) next to them or highlight them (in number 2). Write them in the tally chart below under the column labeled "Favorite." Ask classmates to place a tally mark to show what their favorite is (see holiday example below).

Favorite (your subject)	Tallies (votes by students)
1.	
2.	
3.	
4.	
5.	

Example

Favorite Holiday	Tallies (votes by students)
1. Halloween	1111
2. Christmas	111
3. Hanukkah	11
4. July 4th	1111
5. Thanksgiving	11

4. Create a bar graph using your tally chart data (see number 3). Include a title and labels for axes (horizontal X and vertical Y).

Example

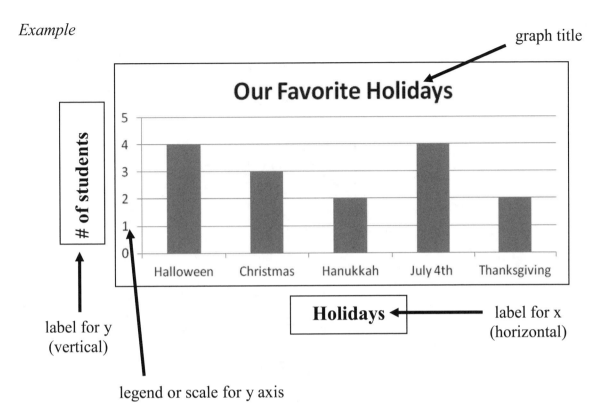

graph title

label for y (vertical)

legend or scale for y axis

label for x (horizontal)

Thinksheet 3.18: Graph Rubric

Criteria	0	1	2
Title	No title	Title present but does not match the graph's purpose	Title matches graph's purpose
Axis (bottom or horizontal)	No axis	Axis included but not specific to graph's content	Axis included and related to graph's content
Axis (side or vertical)	No axis	Axis included but frequency amount chosen is not logical	Axis included and frequency amount is logical
Correctness	Many mistakes	Few mistakes (three to five)	Few or no mistakes (zero to two)
Neatness	Graph is messy	Graph could be neater	Graph is neat

Optional: You can add another row for the legend/scale if you want students to develop an appropriate scale for the graph.

Thinksheet 3.19: African Animal Fun Facts

African Animal Fun Facts

Fun Fact	Zebra	Elephant	Lion
Diet	Herbivore	Herbivore	Carnivore
Height	3-5 ft.	8-13 ft.	4-6 ft.
Weight	440-990 lbs.	5,000-14,000 lbs.	300-500 lbs.
Life Span	25 years	70 years	18 years

Title

A column goes up and down

A row extends across

Directions: Use the table below to answer the questions and fill in the blanks for each sentence.

Carillon Elementary School Lunch Room Drink Sales by Day of the Week

Types of Drinks Sold	Monday	Tuesday	Wednesday
Water	10	20	5
Chocolate milk	30	25	10
Plain milk	10	20	5
Apple juice	20	15	5
Total drinks sold by day	70	80	25

1. How many waters were sold on Tuesday?   _____

2. How many apple juices were sold on Monday?   _____

3. How many drinks (total) were sold on Wednesday?   _____

4. How many plain milks were sold during the three days?   _____

5. Which drink was sold the most during the three days?   _____

6. On _____, a total of 80 drinks were sold.

7. Only 5 apple juices were sold on _____.

8. Thirty chocolate milks were sold on _____.

9. On Wednesday, a total of _____ drinks were sold.

10. On Tuesday, 15 _____ were sold.

Bonus: Create a new question or statement based on the table.

Thinksheet 3.21: Creating a Table

Name: _____

1. Identify three animals you want to find fun facts on. List them below.

   a. _____

   b. _____

   c. _____

2. Choose four facts you want to find out about your animals. Some ideas include: where they live, what they eat, how long they live, how much they weigh, and how tall they are. List the four facts you want to find out below:

   Fact 1: _____

   Fact 2: _____

   Fact 3: _____

   Fact 4: _____

3. Use resources to research your animals. A great website to visit to get some of this information is: http://animals.nationalgeographic.com/animals/facts. Use this blank table to input your information.

Fun Fact	Animal 1	Animal 2	Animal 3
Fact 1			
Fact 2			
Fact 3			
Fact 4			

4. What would be a good title for your table?

   _____

Have your teacher check your facts before creating a final draft of your table.

Thinksheet 3.22: Table Rubric

Criteria	0	1	2
Title	No title	Table is titled but does not match the table's purpose.	Title is included and matches the table's purpose.
Labels for the first row (horizontal)	No labels	Labels are included but do not clearly identify the subjects of the table.	Labels are included and clearly identify subjects of the table.
Labels for the first column (vertical)	No labels	Labels are included but do not describe the subtopics for the subjects of the table.	Labels are included and clearly identify subtopics for subjects of the table.
Correctness	Table has many mistakes.	Few mistakes (three to five).	Few or no mistakes (zero to two).
Neatness	Table is messy.	Table could be neater.	Table is neat.

Thinksheets for
CHAPTER 4

Thinksheet 4.1: Write a Table of Contents

Name _____

Table of Contents   Page

_____   _____

_____   _____

_____   _____

_____   _____

_____   _____

_____   _____

Thinksheet 4.2: Alphabetical Index Sorting Cards

wheels 4, 5	safety 6
helmet 3, 6	tricycle 2
mountain bike 2, 5	road bike 2
brakes 5	chain 5

Index

Topic   Page numbers

_____   _____

_____   _____

_____   _____

_____   _____

_____   _____

_____   _____

_____   _____

Thinksheet 4.4: What Is a Glossary?

Name _____

Title	Where is the glossary (at the beginning, middle, or end of the book)?	What type of information is in the glossary?

Thinksheets for
CHAPTER 5

Thinksheet 5.1: Examples of Text Feature Cards

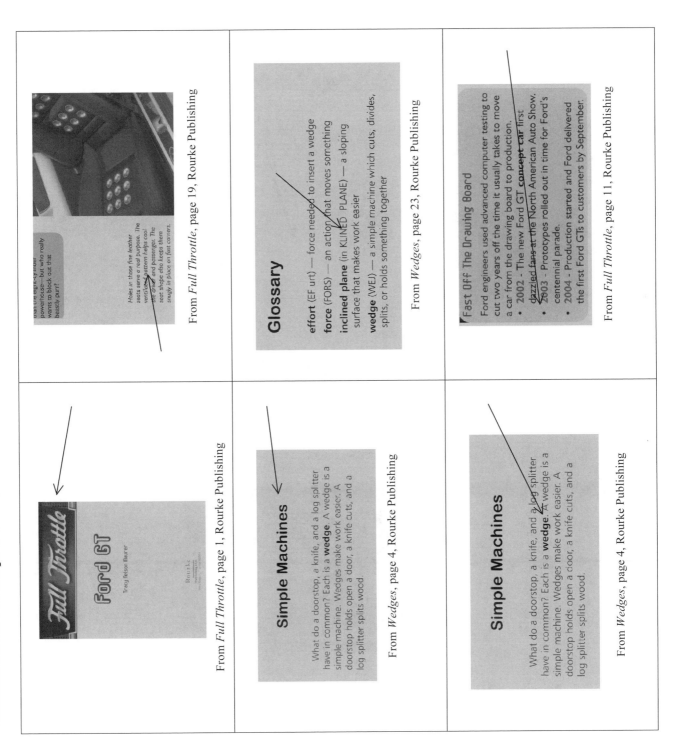

From *Full Throttle*, page 19, Rourke Publishing

Glossary

effort (EF urt) — force needed to insert a wedge

force (FORS) — an action that moves something

inclined plane (in KLINED PLANE) — a sloping surface that makes work easier

wedge (WEJ) — a simple machine which cuts, divides, splits, or holds something together

From *Wedges*, page 23, Rourke Publishing

Fast Off The Drawing Board

Ford engineers used advanced computer testing to cut two years off the time it usually takes to move a car from the drawing board to production.
- 2002 - The new Ford GT concept car first dazzled fans at the North American Auto Show.
- 2003 - Prototypes rolled out in time for Ford's centennial parade.
- 2004 - Production started and Ford delivered the first Ford GTs to customers by September.

From *Full Throttle*, page 11, Rourke Publishing

Ford GT
Trevg Nelson Maurer

Rourke
Publishing LLC

From *Full Throttle*, page 1, Rourke Publishing

Simple Machines

What do a doorstop, a knife, and a log splitter have in common? Each is a **wedge**. A wedge is a simple machine. Wedges make work easier. A doorstop holds open a door, a knife cuts, and a log splitter splits wood.

From *Wedges*, page 4, Rourke Publishing

Simple Machines

What do a doorstop, a knife, and a log splitter have in common? Each is a **wedge**. A wedge is a simple machine. Wedges make work easier. A doorstop holds open a door, a knife cuts, and a log splitter splits wood.

From *Wedges*, page 4, Rourke Publishing

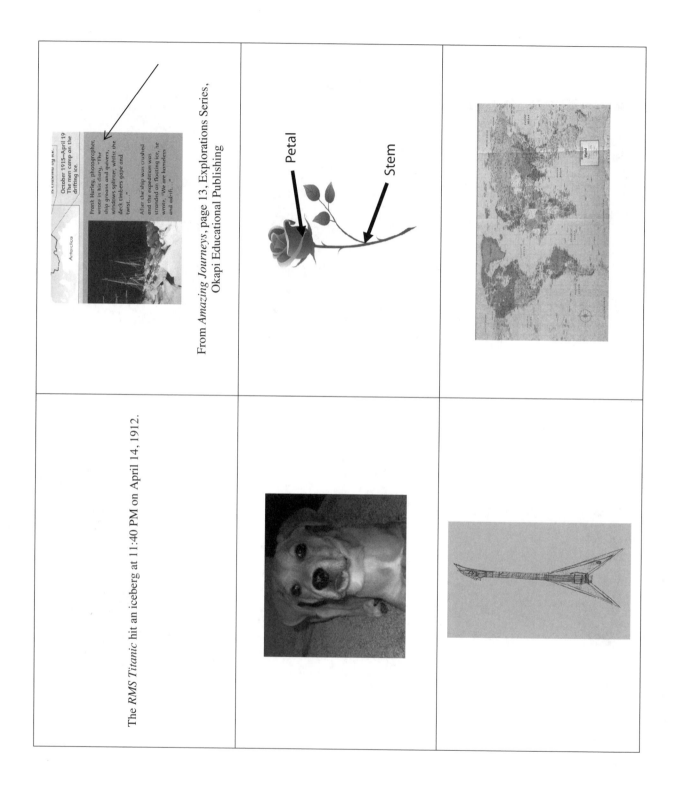

From *Amazing Journeys*, page 13, Explorations Series, Okapi Educational Publishing

October 1915–April 19
The men camp on the drifting ice.

Frank Hurley, photographer, wrote in his diary, "The ship groans and quivers, windows splinter, whilst the deck timbers gape and twist..."

After the ship was crushed and the expedition was stranded on floating ice, he wrote, "We are homeless and adrift..."

Antarctica

Petal

Stem

The *RMS Titanic* hit an iceberg at 11:40 PM on April 14, 1912.

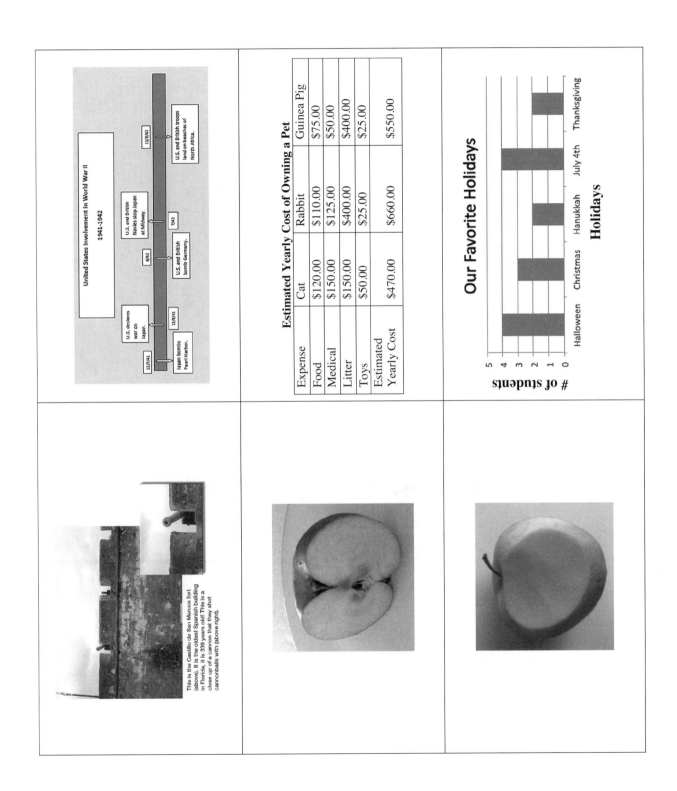

United States Involvement in World War II
1941-1942

12/7/41	Japan bombs Pearl Harbor.
12/8/41	U.S. declares war on Japan.
6/42	U.S. and British bomb Germany.
7/42	U.S. and British Navies stop Japan at Midway.
11/42	U.S. and British troops land on beaches of North Africa.

Estimated Yearly Cost of Owning a Pet

Expense	Cat	Rabbit	Guinea Pig
Food	$120.00	$110.00	$75.00
Medical	$150.00	$125.00	$50.00
Litter	$150.00	$400.00	$400.00
Toys	$50.00	$25.00	$25.00
Estimated Yearly Cost	$470.00	$660.00	$550.00

Our Favorite Holidays

# of students

Halloween   Christmas   Hanukkah   July 4th   Thanksgiving

Holidays

This is the Castillo de San Marcos fort (above). It is the oldest Spanish building in Florida. It is 339 years old! This is a close up of a cannon that they shot cannonballs with (above right).

Table of Contents

From *Wedges*, page 3, Rourke Publishing

Index

From *Wedges*, page 24, Rourke Publishing

Life cycle of the monarch butterfly

eggs — caterpillar — pupa — early stage — pupa — later stage — adult butterfly

From *Amazing Journeys*, pages 4-5, Explorations Series, Okapi Educational Publishing

Glossary

effort (EF urt) — force needed to insert a wedge

force (FORS) — an action that moves something

inclined plane (in KLINED PLANE) — a sloping surface that makes work easier

wedge (WEJ) — a simple machine which cuts, divides, splits, or holds something together

From *Wedges*, page 23, Rourke Publishing

Thinksheet 5.2: Names (Labels) of Text Features

Print Features (Heading)	Graphic Features (Heading)	Organizational Features (Heading)
Title	Drawing	Index
Heading/Subheading	Inset	Glossary
Bold Print	Cutaway	Chart/Table
Table of Contents	Diagram	Sidebar
Pronunciation Guide	Map	Photograph
Italics	Caption	Labeled Diagram
Bullets	Graph	Timeline

Thinksheet 5.3: Text Feature Definitions

The name of a text, usually on the front cover or at the beginning of a chapter	A title at the beginning of a section of text
Words in the text written in a dark and thick print, often in the glossary	A box of extra text to the side of or under the main body of text, often with a shaded background
An explanation that tells how to say a word	Text in a list with a dot or dash in front of each idea
Pictures taken with a camera	A hand-drawn sketch
A picture of something with part of the side missing so we see some of the inside	A small photo, picture, or map inside of or next to a larger picture
A list located at the back of the book that includes specific topics in the book with page numbers	A guide located at the back of the book that lists important words from the text in alphabetical order and tells what those words mean
Numbers or information shown in columns and rows with headings	A series of pictures with captions showing steps or stages
Events on a specific topic listed along a line in the order that they occurred	A list located at the beginning of the text with key topics in the book and their starting page numbers
Data shown as a bar, line, or pie chart	

Thinksheet 5.4: Text Feature T-Chart

Name of text feature	Page number where I found the text feature

Thinksheet 5.5: Print Feature Scavenger Hunt

Name: _____

Print Feature Scavenger Hunt

Directions: In the first column, write the name of the book where you looked for text features. In the other columns, write the page number where you found that text feature in the book.

Title of Book	Title	Heading/Subheading	Bold Print	Italic Print	Caption	Pronunciation Guide	Bullets	Sidebar

Text Features

Thinksheet 5.6: Graphic Feature Scavenger Hunt

Name: _____

Graphic Feature Scavenger Hunt

Directions: In the first column, write the name of the book where you looked for text features. In the other columns, write the page number where you found that text feature in the book.

Text Features

Title of Book	Photograph or Drawing	Inset	Cutaway or Cross-section	Diagram	Map	Graph	Timeline	Chart/Table

Thinksheet 5.7: Organizational Feature Scavenger Hunt

Name: _____

Organizational Feature Scavenger Hunt

Directions: In the first column, write the name of the book where you looked for text features. In the other columns, write the page number where you found that text feature in the book.

	Text Features		
Title of Book	Table of Contents	Index	Glossary

Thinksheet 5.8: Blank Scavenger Hunt

Name: _____

Text Feature Scavenger Hunt

Directions: In the first column, write the name of the book where you looked for text features. In the other columns, write the page number where you found that text feature in the book.

Text Features

Title of Book							

Appendix F
List of Resources on the CD

"I Want a Dog" Picture Book (formatted for printing)
"I Want a Dog" Picture Book (formatted for displaying)

Chapter 1

Table 1.2: Text Feature Definitions and Examples

 = Interactive pdf file

Chapter 2

Thinksheet 2.1: Give Your Book a Title

Thinksheet 2.2: Chapter Title Sort Cards

Thinksheet 2.3: Create a Cover

Thinksheet 2.4: Help! Animals Need to Be Rescued Article

Thinksheet 2.5: Bold and Italic Word Detective

Thinksheet 2.6: Caption Match Sorting Cards

Print Features Activity 7: Flamingo Feather Image

Thinksheet 2.7: Where Does It Fit?

Thinksheet 2.8: Write a Caption

Thinksheet 2.9: Text Bullets

Thinksheet 2.10: Reading Bullets

Thinksheet 2.11: All about Me in Bullets

Thinksheet 2.12: Using Bullets to Summarize

Thinksheet 2.13: Which Sidebar Fits?

Print Features Readers' Theatre Script

Chapter 3

Thinksheet 3.1: Which Picture?

Thinksheet 3.2: Set in What?

Thinksheet 3.3: Inset Hunt

Thinksheet 3.4: Cross-section Hunt

Graphic Features Activity #13: How to Read a Diagram Poster

Thinksheet 3.5: Explain It! Creating a Diagram

Thinksheet 3.6: Diagram Rubric

Graphic Features Activity #17: What Is a Map? Sentence Frame

Thinksheet 3.7: Parts of a Map: What Am I?

Notes:

Notes:

Notes: